The Treaty of Versailles

A Captivating Guide to the Peace Treaty That Ended World War 1 and Its Impact on Germany and the Rise of Adolf Hitler

© Copyright 2020

All Rights Reserved. No part of this book may be reproduced in any form without permission in writing from the author. Reviewers may quote brief passages in reviews.

Disclaimer: No part of this publication may be reproduced or transmitted in any form or by any means, mechanical or electronic, including photocopying or recording, or by any information storage and retrieval system, or transmitted by email without permission in writing from the publisher.

While all attempts have been made to verify the information provided in this publication, neither the author nor the publisher assumes any responsibility for errors, omissions or contrary interpretations of the subject matter herein.

This book is for entertainment purposes only. The views expressed are those of the author alone, and should not be taken as expert instruction or commands. The reader is responsible for his or her own actions.

Adherence to all applicable laws and regulations, including international, federal, state and local laws governing professional licensing, business practices, advertising and all other aspects of doing business in the US, Canada, UK or any other jurisdiction is the sole responsibility of the purchaser or reader.

Neither the author nor the publisher assumes any responsibility or liability whatsoever on the behalf of the purchaser or reader of these materials. Any perceived slight of any individual or organization is purely unintentional.

Free Bonus from Captivating History (Available for a Limited time)

Hi History Lovers!

Now you have a chance to join our exclusive history list so you can get your first history ebook for free as well as discounts and a potential to get more history books for free! Simply visit the link below to join.

Captivatinghistory.com/ebook

Also, make sure to follow us on Facebook, Twitter and Youtube by searching for Captivating History.

Contents

FREE BONUS FROM CAPTIVATING HISTORY (AVAILABLE FOR A LIMITED TIME) 1
INTRODUCTION 3
CHAPTER 1 - FOUNDATIONS 5
CHAPTER 2 - WHAT CAME BEFORE 7
CHAPTER 3 - THE TRUCE AND THE RUN-UP TO VERSAILLES 11
CHAPTER 4 - THE ALLIES 18
CHAPTER 5 - THE FOURTEEN POINTS 42
CHAPTER 6 - THE SCRAMBLED MAP AND PEOPLE OF EUROPE 52
CHAPTER 7 - THE MIDDLE EAST 61
CHAPTER 8 - GERMANY 68
CHAPTER 9 - THE "STAB-IN-THE-BACK" MYTH 74
CHAPTER 10 - THE LEAGUE OF NATIONS FIASCO 94
CONCLUSION 102
SOURCES 104

Introduction

For six months in 1919, from the beginning of January to the end of June, the eyes of much of the world were on the French capital, Paris. The city was accustomed to being at the center of world events. It had seen the rise and fall of the Celts, Romans, and Franks. It had seen Viking raids too many to count, not to mention palace intrigue, revolution, and wars. Paris was perhaps *the* cultural hub of the world from the mid-1600s to the 20th century.

However, its importance has not waned in recent years. The world held its breath when Notre Dame Cathedral in Paris caught fire in April 2019. For many French Catholics, Notre Dame is just as much a part of their faith as communion. The rest of the world watched the cathedral burn, hoping that it would remain standing and that its relics would be saved, as many see it as a symbol of Western civilization and one of the most important centers of cultural and artistic history in the world.

France, besides its inspirational and historic buildings, has played an important role in the world in other ways as well. For centuries, French was the language of diplomacy. The term "lingua franca" is used to describe a language that is universally used to make communication between disparate peoples and languages possible. It literally means "language of the Franks," the tribe after which France is named. Though its literal meaning refers to French, today, the "lingua franca" of diplomacy, economics, and much else is English. Perhaps in fifty to one hundred years, it will be Mandarin Chinese. Only time will tell.

This might seem like an odd set-up, but it demonstrates the central role that France, Paris, and the French have played in world history. And they would play such a role again in 1919, as Paris would be the setting for the diplomatic conference that would put an end to World War I. The treaty that ended the war, also known as the "war to end all wars," was signed at the Palace of Versailles, which had been the home of French kings until 1789 and remains one of the most beautiful structures in the world.

Though the men of Versailles (and they were *overwhelmingly* men) had arrived in Paris to put an end to World War I, by the time the conference ended, the main goal of the diplomats and national leaders had turned into ending wars for all time.

Obviously, that did not work, and as a matter of fact, the end result of the Paris Peace Conference—the Treaty of Versailles—would likely cause more wars than any of its authors could have possibly dreamed of, including World War II.

Chapter 1 – Foundations

In 1919, the victorious powers of World War I met in Paris and its (formerly) royal suburb of Versailles to hammer out a treaty that would put a formal end to the war, which had ended on the battlefield in November 1918. The Treaty of Versailles, which was just one of the many products of the talks between nations, is so important to learn about in order to understand what came after it, as it impacts the world today. For example, the modern Middle East is a construct of the Paris Peace Conference, and the boundaries of the nations as they stand today were artificially constructed by the victorious European powers in 1919. As you likely know, wars have been fought not only over these boundaries but also over many other issues that were decided in France at the beginning of the 20th century.

The matters taken under consideration at the Paris Peace Conference were so numerous and so vast in their scope that no one there could recall a moment in history in which so many powers had come together to discuss the many issues affecting people around the globe.

The only example from history that the leaders and diplomats had to look to for guidance was the talks that took place after the fall of Napoleon in 1814. The talks, which are referred to by historians as the Congress of Vienna, decided matters pertaining to Europe (and only Europe) after the turbulent period of the French Revolution and Napoleon Bonaparte.

The Congress of Vienna established what came to be called the Concert of Europe. In theory, the nations of Europe would act in concert with each other to prevent the rise of another revolutionary power, such as France had been from 1789 to 1815. In very general terms, what the Concert of Europe meant was that the great powers (Britain, Prussia, Austria-Hungary, and Russia) would ensure that conservative forces, which refers to the aristocracy of those nations, would keep radicals from coming to power in Europe again. To this end, the former royal family of France, the Bourbons, was restored. This situation lasted from 1815 to about 1848, which was when liberal revolutions and ideas spread once again through Europe.

In 1919, the Congress of Vienna was the only model the men at the Paris Peace Conference had. It was not enough, for while the wars of the French Revolution and Napoleon had been devastating, they were nothing compared to the scale of death and destruction of the First World War. The men of the Congress of Vienna were dealing with the aftermath of the wars, as well as the impact of the French Revolution, which had changed the way people in Europe looked at government and society. The Paris Peace Conference, on the other hand, was global in its scope and dealt with not only how to put a permanent end to World War I but also how to end war for all time, and that was just one of the hundreds of topics it addressed.

Chapter 2 – What Came Before

What came before the Paris Peace Conference and the Treaty of Versailles was the First World War, the bloodiest and costliest war the European powers (along with Japan, the United States, and the Ottoman Empire) had ever seen. Besides being so destructive physically, the war was destructive in other ways.

Economically, many of the nations of Europe were broke. Even the victors were bankrupt, with one important exception, the United States, which actually came out of the war richer than it had ever been. The expenditures of each nation involved in the war were great. In northern France, the most industrialized part of the nation, many of the factories, mines, and railroads, among other industries had been destroyed or taken to Germany. Belgian industry had been similarly treated. Though Russia was a much less industrialized nation than France or Belgium, the western portion, which had been occupied by the Germans and Austro-Hungarians, suffered in much the same way.

Of course, the loss of manpower was not only tragic to the nation and to the families of the fallen emotionally. Financially, on both a family, local, and national level, most of the dead were in the prime working years, being between sixteen to fifty years old. The deaths of these men would be felt for years after the war, and it would only be exacerbated by the Spanish flu pandemic, which killed anywhere between seventeen to fifty million people worldwide after the war ended, and this pandemic was not helped by the mass immigration from Europe to the United States and elsewhere.

Making matters worse, the victors, especially France and the United Kingdom, were indebted to the United States for what would be tens of billions of dollars today, and it seemed as if they had no way to pay it back.

Aside from the physical and economic losses sustained during the war, the emotional and psychological toll, both on the nations and on individuals, was huge. At the time, enlightened medical professionals were aware that there would be mental repercussions from such a bloody, violent war. Psychology was still in its infancy, but even back then, the most ignorant peasant in the countryside knew that his returning neighbor, friend, or brother was not and was never going to be the same.

World War I was radically different from all other wars before it. Entire libraries can be filled with volumes about how the war changed not only warfare but also politics, among other things. Though wars had been bloody since time began and had gotten progressively bloodier, no one was quite prepared for the deaths in the First World War.

In simple terms, the war was a death factory. World War I was fought with weapons unimaginable even fifty years before. Planes, zeppelins, machine guns, tanks, mass-produced and quick-firing artillery, poison gas—all of these were new, or relatively new, on the battlefield. No one in 1914 was prepared with how quickly men could and would die on the battlefields of World War I.

To give the reader an idea of the nature of the battlefields of the war, especially on the Western Front, in 1916, the British engaged the Germans along the Somme River in northern France. On the first day alone, the British lost 20,000 men, and many of those fell in the first few hours. This was how lethal the combination of newer weapons and old tactics was in World War I.

Another way to demonstrate the magnitude of the battles has to do with the United States. Most Americans know that, even to this day, the American Civil War was the costliest conflict ever fought by the United States. An estimated 600,000 to 750,000 men were killed–more than all of the other wars fought by the US *combined*.

Had World War I continued for much longer than it did, the losses in the Civil War would have been far surpassed, especially since The US only entered the war in 1917. It took months for the bulk of the American army to get to Europe, receive additional training, be equipped, and be deployed. Planning and command issues added to the time it took before the "doughboys," as the American soldiers were called during World War I, the name arising from the ugly buttons on their uniforms that resembled lumps of dough or crude cakes named "doughboys," got into the fighting in any major way.

The first major US offensive took place in late May 1918, more than a full year after President Woodrow Wilson had declared war on the Central Powers, which mainly consisted of Germany, Austria-Hungary, and the Ottoman Empire. Between May and November of 1918 (when the war ended), the US suffered around 120,000 deaths. That took place over a period of a little more than five months. Multiply that number by 9.6, which equals the number of months of the Civil War, and you get a total of 1,152,000. This illustrates the deadly nature of World War I and why the US and many other nations around the world loathed the idea of getting into another war after it.

Though there were significant differences, this story holds true for all of the major participants of the war, not just the Allies. Germany, in particular, was hit hard, for reasons that will become clear. The Americans might have lost a little over 100,000 men, but the other combatants of the war lost a combined total of about nine million. Many European leaders (those of France and Britain, in particular) were not keen on Americans coming over the Atlantic to give them a lecture about not taking revenge.

There are some important points to remember as we go forward. For one, the United States had the benefit of having the Atlantic Ocean between it and Europe. The war did not touch the US, and as such, no fighting took place on its soil. The same holds true for Great Britain, though England did suffer bombing raids during the war (though they were far less deadly than that of World War II), as well as a very high casualty count.

It is also important to note that Belgium and France were the scenes of most of the major battles of the war. Most of Belgium was occupied by the Germans for the entire war, and much of northern France was occupied for most of the conflict as well. The experiences of the Belgians and, more importantly, the French were to set the tone for the peace talks that followed the truce.

Chapter 3 – The Truce and the Run-Up to Versailles

World War I began in the summer of 1914. Its immediate cause was the assassination of Austrian Archduke Franz Ferdinand, the heir to the throne of the Austro-Hungarian Empire, as well as his wife Sophie, but as historians have been saying for years, this was just the "spark" that set off the powder keg that was Europe before 1914.

From the 1870s onward, many people (and not just those in politics and the military) expected a general European war to break out at any time. Rivalries for colonies, the search for political and economic influence (not just in Europe but throughout the world), ethnic hatreds, the desires of some groups to have nations of their own (the Czechs and Slovaks are two of many such examples), rivalries between monarchs (Germany's Kaiser Wilhelm II, England's King George V, and Russia's Tsar Nicholas II were all first cousins who had been compared against each other since their youth), and the infamous alliance system that called for nations to defend their allies in the case of aggression were all factors that led to the war.

The war was fought in Europe, Africa, the Pacific, and parts of Asia. An estimated twenty million people were killed during the war, which was more than any war fought before it. Nations became bankrupt, and empires fell. Entire generations of men were almost completely wiped out. World War I began with marching bands sending men off to win a victory, but it ended with the nations of the world psychologically, physically, and financially ruined.

It was on the eleventh hour of the eleventh day of the eleventh month of 1918 that the fighting of World War I on the Western Front and in the Middle East stopped. The guns had already fallen silent on the Eastern Front the previous year when Vladimir Lenin's Bolsheviks took power in Russia, taking that country out of the war.

When the war ended, Germany and its main allies, Austria-Hungary and the Ottoman Empire, were defeated or on their way to being so. That last phrase is important because, when the war ended, German troops were still in possession of lands in Belgium and France, which they had occupied for most of the war, though they were being pushed back toward their home country by the time hostilities ended. Still, within Germany, there were those in the years to come that could claim that "the German Army did not lose the war. Germany itself was never invaded from east nor west." As you can see on the map below, which includes the occupation of certain areas of Germany after the Treaty of Versailles, Germany had not been invaded during the war.

Illustration 1: Front lines at the end of WWI and occupation zones after Treaty of Versailles. Red arrow indicates British line of march after the treaty. (courtesy nzhistory.govt.nz)

For the other defeated nations, the end of the war was relatively simple: they ceased to exist. Austria-Hungary, once one of the mightiest empires in the world, dissolved under the weight of its multi-ethnic nature, strife, and the desires for freedom among its many minorities. The Habsburg dynasty, which had ruled not only Austria-Hungary but also, at times, many other parts of Europe, finally toppled at the end of World War I, meaning Austria-Hungary was no more. In its place were a group of new nations made up of ancient peoples, although it would not be smooth sailing for these new nations as they had to deal with improvised borders and ethnic hatred, among other issues.

In a similar manner, the Ottoman Empire, whose capital was Constantinople (today's Istanbul) and whose dominant ethnic group was the Turks, fell apart a few years after the war. Their defeat in the war, along with the nation's own set of ethnic and religious problems, tore the once powerful Ottoman Empire apart, resulting in even more changes to the map, many of which are still felt today. Look at the Kurds, for instance. During the Paris Peace Conference, the Great Powers discussed what they should do (if anything) for the Kurds of today's Turkey, Iraq, and Syria. The answer was "not much." While Kurdish leaders lobbied them for an independent "Kurdistan," the Big Three generally believed that, under the auspices of their own colonial/mandate governments in the region, the Kurds would enjoy autonomy and representation in government. Over the course of the next 110 years, the independence and freedom of the Kurds waxed and waned, and they have never had their own country.

So, with the disintegration of the major nations of the Central Powers, this meant that only Germany was left intact. This was an important point, not only for Germany as a nation but for the men who settled the peace terms at Versailles between January 18th, 1919 and January 1920 in Paris.

The Lead-Up to the Paris Peace Conference

The end of the war took nearly everyone by surprise. Among the Allies, the French, British (and their Dominion/Imperial allies, such as Canada, Australia, and New Zealand), and Americans expected the Germans to fight until Germany (or a large portion of it) was occupied. They knew from prisoners and spies that Germany's fortunes were waning and that the situation within Germany was grim and getting worse, but the Germans at the front were still there, still fighting, and they were still in possession of large chunks of Allied territory.

Amazingly, the population of Germany believed the war was still going well or, at the very least, "all right." The British navy had imposed a blockade on the country, which cut deep into its food supply, and people were beginning to go hungry in Germany. Protests were a regular occurrence, but many people believed that part of the reason for this hunger was because the troops needed to be fed first. They did not know or chose not to believe how bad the situation on the front was.

It was easy to cling to these beliefs for a number of reasons. The main reason was that the press was tightly controlled in Germany. This was true in peacetime and doubly true during the war. Media censorship was not what it became under the Nazis beginning in 1933, but Germany was an authoritarian monarchy that monitored the press closely. Though Germany was ostensibly a constitutional parliamentary democracy, under Kaiser ("Caesar" or "Emperor") Wilhelm II, it was more of a police state than an actual democracy, and the military was at the top of the food chain, so to speak. This was especially true during the war.

Therefore, for the most part, the German public had to hear what was happening in the war from their papers and their leaders, and they were saying that Germany was winning the war. Yes, the papers said there had been setbacks at times, but the German Empire was still in possession of large swathes of Russia and Ukraine, and it was holding onto its gains on the Western Front.

Some people, of course, knew the truth, but many of them chose to duck their heads in the sand. It was safer, not only physically (because voicing a contrary opinion could be incredibly dangerous) but also psychologically. It was hard to admit that after such tremendous sacrifice and loss that Germany was losing the war. Germany didn't lose wars, especially to France, at least not since the fall of Napoleon Bonaparte and the successful defeat of his nephew Napoleon III in 1870.

The official line from the government, and at this point that essentially meant the military, was that Germany was just one great effort away from complete victory. Of course, that had been said before, most notably in the spring of 1918 when General Erich Ludendorff (one of the two men who essentially ran the war effort, the other being Field Marshal Paul von Hindenburg) launched an offensive incorporating new tactics that were designed to knock France out of the war. For a variety of reasons, mostly due to heroic resistance by the French and the British, the offensive failed. At that point, most of the German high command knew that it was just a matter of time before the war was lost, especially with the United States now in the picture, as there was now a strong possibility of millions of US soldiers arriving in Europe shortly.

Since the German high command knew the war was lost, they put out feelers for peace in the fall of 1918. Many of the higher officers, especially those privy to the big picture (such as supplies, manpower, and intelligence), also knew that Germany could not hold out for long. Leading opposition politicians knew it too—the people were beginning to go hungry because of the British blockade, among other things. Many of the more cognizant foot soldiers knew it as well, especially those who kept in contact with their friends and relatives back home.

But many of the normal German foot soldiers did not know it or chose to ignore the signs. If they had had their eyes open, they would have realized that they were slowly being pushed back toward Germany. They also would have realized that the men coming to the front lines now were either more like boys or old men, as the manpower pool was dwindling rapidly. Another problem that was literally staring them in the face was that the Allies seemed to be getting stronger, not weaker. More supplies were rolling in from

America, and more and more "doughboys" were being seen on the lines or behind it.

Many of the youngsters heading to the front in the summer and fall of 1918 would become sergeants and officers when Adolf Hitler rebuilt the army in the 1930s. In 1918, though, they had gone to the front, and then, all of a sudden (seemingly), the war was over, and Germany had lost. In their minds, something wasn't quite right.

In the summer of 1918, the Allies had begun the offensive that essentially led to the end of the war. The Germans fell back, then fell back again. The generals of the Central Powers often discussed asking the Allies for a truce. In late September, one of Germany's last extant allies, Bulgaria, signed an armistice with the Allies. At that point, General Ludendorff, overburdened with the war effort and the idea of losing the war, collapsed and had a mental breakdown. At this point, Hindenburg took the reins.

By this time, the German Navy, which was ordered to sail out and try to defeat the British blockade (a lost cause if there ever was one), revolted in the ports of northern Germany. Soon, the entire country was in rebellion, demanding for the war to end. The opposition in the Reichstag (the German parliament) declared a new government, and Kaiser Wilhelm II was forced to abdicate. He fled to Holland, which was neutral in World War I, and died there in 1941.

The new German government, with Hindenburg's blessing, appointed a royal as an emissary to the Allies to seek out terms for a ceasefire. This was not to be a surrender, at least in the eyes of the Germans, but a truce until a more permanent peace could be secured. The Allied leader they approached was US President Woodrow Wilson.

Why Wilson? Both the British and French (especially the French, who had lost territory and over a million and a half men, along with millions more casualties) were bent on revenge. The US had entered the war late, and their casualty count was minimal compared to the other Allies. Also, they had not been invaded, and virtually no American civilians had lost their lives. Besides this, there were

Wilson's "Fourteen Points," his plan for ending war. And it was not just this war that Wilson wanted to end—he sought to end all of them, forever.

Chapter 4 – The Allies

Leaders from around the world came to Paris in 1919. World War I was, after all, a world war, and it was fought not only in Europe but also Africa, the Middle East, and, to a smaller degree, parts of eastern Asia. Almost all of these nations had declared war against the Central Powers, which included European nations such as Portugal and countries afar afield as Brazil and others in Latin America, who essentially wanted to prove to the United States that they would be good business partners. Some of these nations were able to secure better loans and business deals at Paris, as well as later on, but in the main, nations, such as Brazil that came to Paris hoping for gains of some kind on their continent (which had nothing to do with the war), were left in the cold.

Japan was represented as well, having joined the war against Germany. They did this not because they were overly friendly with the Allies but because they saw a chance to seize relatively unguarded German territories in the Pacific and China. For their part, the Allies would not have to waste resources in Asia to take these German territories, most of which were worthless to them.

As one can see, when the Paris peace talks opened in the fall of 1919, virtually the whole world was represented, including not only nations but also representatives from ethnic groups without a country and colonies hoping for more autonomy or even independence.

When all was said and done, though, the men who truly counted and crafted the Treaty of Versailles (along with their staffs of hundreds) were the "Big Four." These were French Prime Minister Georges Clemenceau, British Prime Minister David Lloyd George, Italian Prime Minister Vittorio Orlando, and last but not least US President Woodrow Wilson. In actuality, although Orlando and Italy did have a say and played quite a role in the war, he and his country played a relatively minor part in comparison with the other three.

Woodrow Wilson

In December 1918, when President Woodrow Wilson arrived in France, people went wild. For those of you old enough to remember Frank Sinatra, Elvis, or the Beatles, it was like that. Wilson was the 1918 version of a rock star. His image was everywhere: posters, paintings, newspapers, books, plates, you name it. For the people of France and of Europe in general, Wilson was the "American savior."

Illustration 2: Wilson arrives in Europe, the first sitting US president to visit Europe while in office

It wasn't just Wilson that people were going crazy for. It was America. Many have called the 20th century the "American Century." America's economic, cultural, military, and political reach was unparalleled in the 20th century, and it all really began with World War I, Woodrow Wilson, and the Paris Peace Conference.

Emigration from Europe to the US had grown almost every year in the late 19th and early 20th centuries. People all over the European continent wanted a better life, especially one in which they were free from autocrats and traditional ruling classes. This was truer for the immigrants from Eastern Europe, where governments were feared and not chosen by the people in any way. Of course, people from all over Europe and the world flocked to the United States for economic opportunities, but for many of those who remained in Europe, the arrival of Woodrow Wilson signaled (or at least they hoped) a shift in the politics of the past and the dawning of a bright new future.

To them, Wilson represented not only dreams of political and economic freedom, but he also represented the country that had, in effect, ended World War I. Now, it must be remembered that the American troops did precious little fighting in comparison to that of its allies. Britain, France, Russia, and their smaller allies (such as Serbia, Greece, and Belgium) had lost millions of men. The fighting that killed them had gone on for four long years before the arrival of the Americans on the front.

While the American effort at the end of the war certainly did put pressure on the German front lines, the threat (to Germany) and the promise (to the Allies) was American potential. By the end of the war, over a million US soldiers were in Europe, and at least a million more were getting ready back home, with more behind them. America was funding the Allies' war effort almost completely by 1916, and if anything, it was richer at the end of the war than it was before the conflict began. The German high command knew it was just a matter of time before the weight of American industry and manpower forced an end to the war, and they decided they might get a better deal if they approached the Allies sooner rather than later, especially if they approached Wilson.

We briefly went over the reasons why the Germans went to Wilson, but it's also important to discuss Wilson, the man. Though he was propelled into the spotlight due to his presidency at Princeton University and the governorship of New Jersey, Wilson was a Southerner. As a matter of fact, he was the first Southerner to be elected president since 1848 (Andrew Johnson, a Tennessean, became president after the death of Abraham Lincoln).

This presents an interesting window on Wilson's personality. In one of his more famous speeches, one which he aimed at the many ethnic groups of Europe who were dominated by others, he called for what has become known as the "self-determination of people"—in other words, the right of ethnic groups or minorities to have a say in or to form their own governments.

Still, it should be remembered that Wilson was a product of his time and background. Born in Virginia in October 1856 and raised in Georgia during the Civil War and Reconstruction, he, like many others of his time, looked down upon and discriminated against African Americans. As president of Princeton, Wilson issued edicts segregating dormitories, locker rooms, and many other areas of campus life, despite the fact that Princeton was a Northern university. As president of the United States, many black leaders met with Wilson and pressured him to do something about the abysmal conditions for African Americans in the South. Wilson argued with them and then saw them removed from the White House, doing nothing in response.

His famous Fourteen Points speech in 1918, setting out a plan he believed could end World War I, included a statement about colonial peoples having a say in their governments, yet he himself refused to listen to Filipino, Puerto Rican, and other representatives from various American possessions.

Wilson also oftentimes spoke of the European predilection for war and interference in the politics of other nations, yet during his administration, the United States became involved in a low-level war in Mexico, occupied Nicaragua, and sent American troops to Panama, Cuba, and Honduras.

However, Wilson was a brilliant scholar, and his papers on international relations, history, and politics won awards and got him recognition not only in academic circles but in political circles as well. When he ran for governor of New Jersey in 1910, he had never held elected office. As a man with connections to New Jersey's Democratic political machine, Wilson was essentially appointed as the nominee and won the election based not only on his academic reputation but also on his promises of installing progressive reforms in New Jersey, a state known for corruption and big business abuses. At this time in American history, "progressivism" was seen as a reaction to the rampant abuse of big business and political machines over American economic and political life.

After only two years as governor of New Jersey, Wilson was nominated as the Democratic candidate for president. His opponents were incumbent Republican William Howard Taft and Theodore Roosevelt, the former president and the candidate of the new and progressive "Bull Moose Party." The election was essentially a two-man race between Roosevelt and Wilson, with Taft winning only Utah and Vermont. Roosevelt's entry into the race likely cost the Republicans the presidency, though, and Wilson became the 28th president of the United States of America.

Wilson, despite having had only limited experience in elected office, did have a number of things going for him. He understood American politics, as he had written extensively on the subject. He also knew how to play Congress and how to get things done. Despite his bookish appearance, Wilson was a good speaker who could fire up a crowd, and in 1912, crowds were ready to be fired up by a new face who believed in progressive ideals. Wilson had a genuine desire to make people's lives better. Though he was prejudiced against African Americans and believed in segregation, he disliked the Ku Klux Klan (at that time, the Ku Klux Klan enjoyed incredible popularity not just in the South but in the Midwest) and was insulted by the violence against blacks. A blind spot in his logic kept Wilson from seeing that his belief in segregation helped to encourage violence. Still, Wilson did help to improve labor relations and conditions in the US, and he addressed some of the worst abuses of big business.

Wilson was pious, as he was the son of a minister, intelligent, and politically savvy. He was also narrow-minded in many areas, and despite his broad knowledge of American politicians, he was quite ignorant of foreign affairs and geography, which would get him into trouble in Paris. Wilson's other big flaw was his arrogance, which stemmed from a strange conviction that he was always right. He surrounded himself with yes-men (some very capable, for sure, but still yes-men) and would not brook being corrected, even when it was clear to everyone that he was in the wrong.

For example, while he understood that the United States was the emerging power of the world, he also underestimated the wealth and power of the United Kingdom, especially its navy. Additionally, he did not fully comprehend the importance of that navy and the colonies it linked together to the survival of Great Britain. Commenting on the issue at a social gathering at the beginning of the conference, Wilson told a French diplomat, "If England insisted on maintaining naval dominance after the war, the United States could and would show her how to build a navy!"

And while Wilson shared many Americans' admiration for Great Britain's power, wealth, and influence, that admiration was also tinged with a bit of jealousy and the knowledge that England was the nation America had fought against for its independence (two times if you count the War of 1812). At Buckingham Palace for a royal reception, Wilson admonished a British official, letting him know exactly what he thought of talk of "cousins separated by a common language." "You must not speak of us who come over here as cousins, still less as brothers; we are neither."

Of course, some of this was necessary. The United States, like the new kid in the neighborhood, had to let it be known that it would not be pushed around. But for Wilson, this was not all show. He was like this with almost everyone. It is important to note that he did not take any Republicans with him on his peace mission, and he also did not seek their advice before he left. By the time the Treaty of Versailles was ready for ratification in 1920, the Republicans were in control of the Senate, and they were not in the mood to give Wilson a gift.

There was one man that Wilson treated somewhat like an equal, and that was Colonel Edward M. House. House was not really a colonel; he actually had no military experience whatsoever, but he was an influential Southerner and was bestowed that honorific title as many important Southerners were at the time.

House was an extremely successful Texas businessman and mover and shaker in local politics. He was small and had been sickly as a child, but he was exceedingly intelligent and quick-witted. Throughout his life, House admittedly preferred being "the man behind the scenes" who influenced events, and that's what he did under Wilson, whom he had met when he moved from Texas to New York to expand his business and political reach. Realizing that Wilson had a good chance of being elected governor of New Jersey in 1912, House joined his campaign in 1911 and stuck by Wilson from then on.

House was instrumental in helping Wilson navigate national politics and getting him elected as president in 1912. From the beginning of Wilson's administration, House was the man with the power to make things happen. He was given an apartment inside the White House and was the only person to have access to Wilson whenever he wanted it, though it should be noted that he did not hold a formal office, much like Harry Hopkins twenty years later under Franklin Delano Roosevelt. It was only late in Wilson's administration, when Wilson's second wife (his first wife Ellen died in 1914) waged a campaign against him, that House began to lose influence with the president.

Wilson, who for most of his life had been an island unto himself, told House, "You are the only person with whom I can discuss everything...but you are the only person to whom I can make an entire clearance of my mind." As the Europeans in Paris were to learn, if you wanted to change Wilson's mind about something, you needed to go through House first.

Still, Wilson was his own man and made no bones about letting people know it, even when confronted with clear evidence that proved him wrong. And when confronted with the sharp, skilled, and tough personalities of Europe, especially David Lloyd George of Great Britain and Georges Clemenceau of France, Wilson was out of his depth.

David Lloyd George

In many ways, David Lloyd George was Winston Churchill's political mentor. Churchill, while at times strenuously argued with the older man, respected and admired Lloyd George and his quick mind. Think about that for a moment: Churchill, one of the towering figures of the 20th century (and most Americans forget, if they know at all, that he played an exceedingly important role in World War I, as well as in World War II), looked up to and took many political cues and lessons from David Lloyd George.

Illustration 3: Lloyd George before the breakout of WWI. Many people commented on the devilish twinkle in his eyes, especially the ladies, whom he was also quite fond of.

The two could not have been more different—at least on the surface. Churchill was a member of one of the oldest and most influential aristocratic families in England. His father had held every important cabinet post except one—prime minister. His ancestor was Lord Marlborough, who had defeated the armies of France at Blenheim in 1704. Winston Churchill was born in Blenheim Palace, which was Marlborough's home in England and named after his famous victory. Churchill's mother was American and as close to royalty as Americans in the late 19th century could get. Jennie came from the Jerome family, which was one of the wealthiest families in New York at the time (Jerome Avenue in New York City is named for them, as are many other landmarks). Winston Churchill wanted for nothing growing up, at least materially. Emotionally is another story.

David Lloyd George, on the other hand, wasn't English. He was Welsh. To many in the English upper classes, the Welsh were sort of poorer cousins, rough and tumble types from the countryside and the coal mines that dotted their land. Lloyd George's parents were definitely not aristocrats, and they were not rich. His father, William George, was a schoolmaster who died when David was only one year old. After that happened, he was raised by his mother and her brother, Richard Lloyd, who was a shoemaker and an avid follower of the Liberals of the time. Richard's influence on David was so great that the young man took on his last name.

Lloyd George was born in January 1863. Politics in the latter half of the 19th century in Great Britain was dominated by a struggle between Liberal and Conservative ideas. In this case, Conservative ideas meant keeping the class-conscious status quo and allowing businesses to run free in search of profits. Conversely, Liberal politicians of the day pressed for more rights and access to better jobs, politics, and much else for the common people of England.

Many of these struggles centered around labor and the reform of the workplace. Great Britain was the first industrial power in the world. Britain enjoyed the fruits of being first, such as new markets and more capital, but it was also the first to suffer from the rather horrid side-effects of industrialization. By the late 19th century, *some* of the worst abuses had been improved, but the workplaces of 19th- and early 20th-century Britain were far from ideal. It was dirty, unsafe, and unequal, with workers having very little say in their livelihoods and lives. For David Lloyd George, his uncle and people like them saw that changes were desperately needed.

David Lloyd George first became a lawyer, then a journalist, working on cases that reformed the laws of land ownership and access, as well as cases that helped to form labor unions among farmers at a time when this could have been detrimental to one's physical well-being. Lloyd George soon saw that the most effective way to promote change was in politics. He first became involved in the local county council and made a name for himself regionally, and in 1890, he stood for election to Parliament for the city of Caernarvon and kept that seat for the next *fifty-five years.*

Lloyd George became a national figure in the early 1900s when the British were fighting the Dutch Boers in South Africa in a long, drawn-out, and bloody war. Lloyd George was vocal in his opposition against the war, which was an unpopular position at the time, but his courage to speak out gained him both respect and notoriety. As a result, when the Liberals came to power in 1905, Lloyd George was made the president of the Board of Trade, the branch of government (at the time) concerned with industry and commerce. Within the richest nation on the planet, this was an important post.

As the head of the Board of Trade, Lloyd George became nationally known, and in 1908, he became chancellor of the exchequer, the British equivalent of the American secretary of the treasury. Among the many changes that Lloyd George pushed through, the most notable was the National Insurance Act, which was one of the industrialized world's first social security systems.

When World War I began, Lloyd George became the important head of the Ministry of Munitions, overseeing war production. Throughout 1914 and 1915, Lloyd George managed the ministry and the United Kingdom's war effort with great success, navigating labor disputes, money shortages, allocation of resources, and more. When the coalition government of Prime Minister Herbert Asquith fell in 1916, Lloyd George succeeded him, and he was the only Liberal in a cabinet of Conservatives.

It's not hard to understand why Churchill admired Lloyd George. The Welshman was incredibly intelligent and an unbelievably skilled debater. Early in his political career, he was told to defend a certain point in an upcoming debate. Given the wrong information, Lloyd George managed to successfully argue for a position his party was against. During the debate, he was given the correct information, and before the debate was through, he had completely reversed his position—and won the debate.

Lloyd George was a very shrewd politician and could see through to the heart of the matter very quickly, but he was frequently brusque while doing so. His manners, while polite for today's political world, were on the rough side for Great Britain of the early 1900s, and his attitude alienated more than a few people.

He also was surprisingly ignorant about the rest of the world. While he was an able defender of British interests, he frequently got locations of colonies and countries wrong, and this showed up time and again in Paris in 1919. Still, for the most part, this did not matter, for when it came to Woodrow Wilson, he was dealing with a geopolitical neophyte. But when it came to Georges Clemenceau of France, he was not.

Georges Clemenceau

Clemenceau was known as "The Tiger," sometimes, "The Tiger of France." He was given this nickname, which he liked immensely, before the war, when he was noted for his toughness in dealing with both political opponents and seemingly intractable problems. By November 1918, after he had been the prime minister of France for a year and had seen the country and its people through a very grim time of the war and into its victorious last stages, he became known as "The Father of Victory."

Illustration 4: Clemenceau in the years just before WWI

Clemenceau had a wife, an American student named Mary Plummer whom he had met while teaching in the United States, and, like many leading Frenchmen of the time, also had a mistress, but his one great love was France. He had dedicated his life to the country as a young man and had served in the government in a variety of different positions, including having been prime minister from 1906 to 1909 during a time of great unrest in the country.

Clemenceau was born in a very religious, very conservative part of France, but he grew up in a liberal household and was brought up with a great disdain for the Catholic Church. While this was unusual in this part of France, known as the Vendée, France itself had been in a sort of ideological and religious war with itself since the French Revolution of 1789, and religion was one of the main issues of this "war." Early in life, Clemenceau was a medical doctor, as was his father, but he became a teacher when he realized that the practice of medicine didn't speak to him.

Clemenceau's father, Benjamin, had been a political activist all his life, and Georges followed in his father's footsteps. Before leaving for the United States in 1865, he had founded a newspaper in Paris in 1861. This paper, and others he ran (sometimes single-handedly, taking on all the positions himself), were almost always stirring the pot. Clemenceau was a staunch fighter for what he saw as the ideals of the French Republic as first announced in the early days of the French Revolution; he believed there needed to be a separation between church and state, fair treatment for the working classes, and anti-corruption in the government.

His nickname, "The Tiger," was given to him for his penchant for attacking (and sometimes tearing down) governmental cabinets. As is so often the case in parliamentary democracies with a multi-party system, any shift in the balance of power could lead to new elections, and Clemenceau was instrumental in weakening many governments when he believed they were incompetent or corrupt.

He remained in the United States for over four years, working for a time in New York City and then becoming a teacher at an all-girls academy in Connecticut, where he met Plummer. He returned to France in 1870 when the Franco-Prussian War was raging.

The Franco-Prussian War formed not only Clemenceau but a whole generation of Frenchmen. To understand France in the years before World War I and the role France played in the formation of the Treaty of Versailles, it's important to understand this war, which damaged not only France geographically but psychologically as well.

The Franco-Prussian War was the last in a series of three wars fought by the dominant German state of Prussia in order to unite all of the German-speaking states together into one nation. Many people do not realize this, but Germany is a rather new nation—it was founded in 1871 as a result of these wars and especially due to the defeat of France.

Through a series of brilliant political maneuvers, Prussian Prime Minister Otto von Bismarck brought on wars with Denmark (1864) and Austria-Hungary (1866) in order to remove their influence in the German states and principalities, which numbered in the hundreds, in the north and south. Winning against Denmark was expected, but many around the world expected the war with Austria-Hungary to be long and perhaps result in a Prussian defeat. It was not long, and the Prussians actually won.

Four years later, Bismarck set his eyes on removing French influence in the German states in the west, and he skillfully played French emperor Napoleon III (Napoleon Bonaparte's nephew, who ruled from 1848 to 1870) for a fool and maneuvered him into declaring war on Prussia. France, at the time, was seen as the strongest land power in Europe, but the Prussians, through the use of new tactics, new weapons, and better training and leadership, outfought the French and defeated them in short order.

During that short conflict, Paris was under siege, and it was to Paris that Georges Clemenceau returned from the US. For five months, between 1870 and 1871, Paris suffered from famine, disease, and political strife while the Prussians besieged the city. Finally, the French could take no more and asked for peace.

As a result, the German-speaking states of today's western Germany united with Prussia and the other German states, and thus, Germany was born. Not only that, but the bilingual area of the states of Alsace and Lorraine (frequently referred to as just Alsace-Lorraine) were ceded to Germany. This relatively large area west of the traditional French-German border area near or on the Rhine River was historically significant to the French, as Charlemagne's capital of Aachen was nearby, and it was economically very rich.

To the French, ceding Alsace-Lorraine was a national humiliation. Worse, the agreements that both united Germany and gave Alsace-Lorraine to the Germans were signed at the Palace of Versailles, one of France's great and most historic buildings and the center of the French kingdom for centuries.

In 1940, after the defeat of France by Hitler, Churchill spoke to the French nation and included some history from the Franco-Prussian War. He quoted Léon Gambetta, a prominent French politician in the late 1800s, who told Frenchmen when they thought about 1871 to "think of it always, speak of it never." The whole

Franco-Prussian episode, which was a political and military humiliation, gave birth to an entire French political movement named "revanchism"—"revenge."

Though Clemenceau was not at the forefront of the revanchist movement, he developed an implacable dislike of Germany and all things German. Let's just say it: He *hated* Germany, and like most Frenchmen (and women) of the time, he was determined to not only return Alsace-Lorraine to France but to do everything possible to weaken and humiliate Germany at every opportunity until that was done.

From the 1870s until World War I and beyond, Clemenceau spent most of his life in politics. He also founded newspapers that espoused his views and the views of those who agreed with him. Politically, the Tiger was on the left but not the far left. He saw widespread abuses of working people by big business and saw great corruption and abuse of power in the military, and he wanted to fix that.

Already a national figure by the late 1800s, Clemenceau was important in bringing down the Boulangist movement, which rallied behind an ultra-nationalist general who had aspirations of military dictatorship named Georges Boulanger, and Clemenceau also joined with famed writer Émile Zola in his defense of Alfred Dreyfus, the French officer of Jewish descent who was (falsely) accused of being a traitor in the pay of Germany.

By the time World War I broke out, Clemenceau had held a variety of political positions, including prime minister, but he was out of power when the war began. When the war started, Clemenceau's paper was censored under wartime restrictions for reportedly criticizing the war effort and the government's ineffectiveness and lack of transparency. Throughout the war, he criticized the French war effort when it was needed.

In November 1917, after a disastrous year that included widespread mutinies of French troops at the front, Clemenceau became prime minister again. Almost immediately, he fired incompetent generals, changed some draconian rules (which pleased the disheartened French soldiers), and refined the supply process. He improved the alliance with the British and later the United States, though, like Lloyd George, Clemenceau was to develop a personal dislike for Woodrow Wilson.

At the Paris Peace Conference in 1919/20, Clemenceau's first priority was making sure that Germany could never again threaten France. Everything else was secondary to this goal.

Vittorio Orlando

Illustration 5: Orlando (second from right) talking with Lloyd George. Next in line is Clemenceau then Wilson

In one of the most famous photographs taken at the Paris Peace Conference, Wilson, Clemenceau, and Lloyd George are pictured with another man. That man is Vittorio Orlando, and he was the prime minister of Italy during World War I.

Italy had fought a costly war against Austria-Hungary, which was sometimes helped by large numbers of German troops—one being the future German hero Erwin Rommel, in the borderlands between Italy and the Austro-Hungarian Empire. Much of the fighting took place in the mountains, and while most people know that the Western Front of World War I was a particularly brutal and unpleasant place, the mountains of Italy and Austria-Hungary were as well. Italy lost an estimated half a million men in the war, and most of this fighting took place in a very small and congested area along its borders.

Orlando was in Paris to make that the other powers recognized that without the Italian forces holding down hundreds of thousands of enemy troops, the war could have been much worse, as those enemy soldiers could have been sent to the Western Front, perhaps to great effect. He also wanted the French, British, and Americans to know that Italy, just like many other European powers before the war, was an imperial power, with interests in Africa and other parts of the world, and it demanded representation. Orlando and the Italians also wanted a share of the now-defunct Austro-Hungarian Empire, specifically the coastal lands opposite the Italian Peninsula along the Adriatic Sea and northward into the Alps.

Orlando was a Sicilian, and he was born in 1860 on that island before Italy was a country (it unified in 1866). Italian politics in the late 1800s and into the 20th century was dominated by men from the central and northern parts of the country. People like Orlando, who came from the south, be it Sicily or from the heel and toe of the country (Calabria), were looked down upon as peasants and backward. They were also suspected of being criminals, and even after Orlando made a name for himself in national politics, he was accused of having ties to the Mafia. Still, for a Sicilian to rise to become prime minister meant that Orlando was a very able and astute politician.

He entered politics in the late 1890s and began rising through the government ranks, holding a variety of cabinet positions before the outbreak of World War I. When the war broke out in 1914, Orlando supported Italy's entry into it, and he became prime minister in late 1917, about the same time that Clemenceau became head of the French state.

Like Clemenceau, Orlando was presented with a variety of problems, including incompetent power-hungry generals and an ill-equipped and poorly supplied army on the verge of mutiny. Like the Tiger, Orlando fired generals and improved conditions for the Italian soldiers.

However, at the Paris Peace Conference after the war, it soon became apparent that the Big Four was to become the "Big Three," as Wilson, Lloyd George, and Clemenceau thought of Italy as a junior partner; after all, they did not fight against Germany directly, and their record in battle was mixed at best.

Everyone else

Though it is a rather dismissive term to use for a section heading, the Paris Peace talks really were, for the most part, talks between France, Britain, and the United States. Those are the nations that "laid down the law," so to speak. However, that does not mean that the other nations present, especially what might be called the "secondary powers," did not have a say or some influence, either overtly or behind the scenes.

There were over thirty nations represented in Paris, and there was also a large number of representatives from colonial and minority peoples who wished to have their voices heard, but for the purposes of this book, let's stick with some of the larger ones.

Japan

Japan did not join World War I on the Allied side because of any great affinity for the Allied nations, the Allied cause, or a love for Western democracies (though it was ostensibly a parliamentary democracy, Japan still had a powerful emperor, even though Emperor Taishō was weak compared to others, and a military-industrial complex with increasing influence). No, Japan's aim in joining against Germany was simple: the German armed forces guarding its Pacific/Asian interests would be weak, and Germany was not going to be able to reinforce it. Japan "offered" to keep those forces occupied so the Allies didn't have to weaken their European forces and send them around the world.

When World War I ended, the Japanese were interested in two things, one of which was rather admirable. The first was gaining control of German concessions in China and small island chains in the Pacific. The second thing the Japanese wanted was an announcement incorporated into the final treaty that all races were equal. They got the first, but they didn't get the second.

Japan, which began World War II by attacking China in the 1930s, already had its eyes on the rich resources of China in World War I. Taking control of valuable German-controlled areas would increase their footprint in China and allow them to gain access to more natural resources/food, which Japan was lacking.

The island chains in the Pacific (they will sound familiar to any World War II buff—the Marshalls, Marianas, the Carolines, and Palau) would provide Japan with greater access to fish but also allow them to extend their naval reach almost halfway across the Pacific. Since the turn of the century, the United States, Great Britain, and Australia on one side, with Japan on the other, had all been making war plans for conflict in the Pacific, and the control of these islands was key. However, in 1919, the Allied thinking was that Japan could have these small relatively worthless islands for the little fighting they did in World War I. But other nations had their eyes on them as well.

Australia and New Zealand

Australia and New Zealand were both ostensibly possessions of the United Kingdom, but by 1919, they had been Dominion states of the British Empire for twelve years. This meant that they were independent in almost every important way, but they still owed allegiance to the British Crown.

For its part, Australia wanted control of (formerly) German New Guinea, the huge island to its north. Already suspicious of Japan's aims, Australian Prime Minister Billy Hughes insisted on control of this resource-rich island as a buffer against possible Japanese aggression.

Hughes was perfectly Australian about his aims and about his dislike for Woodrow Wilson, whom he hated (the feeling was mutual). At one point during the Paris talks, it seemed to Hughes that Wilson was digging in his heels about Australia gaining any benefit from its very costly involvement in the war, with Australia suffering between 60,000 to 70,000 dead and hundreds of thousands wounded.

At one point, Hughes used an underhanded trick to get his way. The talks were supposed to be secret, as most of the powers agreed to not talk to the press unless it was an approved press conference in which only generalities were discussed or if they had all agreed that it was important to release some information.

On January 29th, 1919, a British newspaper, the *Daily Mail*, ran an article in which it claimed that President Wilson was forcing the British and Dominion powers to give up their important strategic positions due to Wilson's narrow-minded ideas about world peace. The content of the article made it clear to the men participating in the peace talks that the source of the information was the Australian prime minister, who had, in fact, contacted the newspaper.

The next morning, Hughes and the Big Four met in Paris. David Lloyd George was very angry because the article undercut his relationship with Wilson, which was already rocky, and if Wilson felt that the article exposed Great Britain's true feelings, much could be in jeopardy.

On top of all that, Wilson's war aims, which we will discuss shortly, included an eventual elimination of colonies. In the meantime, those territories that weren't given immediate independence were to become "mandates" of the future League of Nations, and they would be governed internationally until it was decided the territory could govern itself.

Of course, Wilson was furious, and he let Hughes know it in both words and actions. He was rude to the Australian, cutting him off, ignoring him, and raising his voice. To Lloyd George, who knew Hughes much better, this was the wrong way to go about dealing with the problem. The situation was compounded by Hughes's deafness, which was helped a bit by a large hearing aid, but sometimes Hughes used his deafness to irritate people.

Wilson loudly asked Hughes, "Am I to understand that if the whole civilized world asks Australia to agree to a mandate in respect to these islands, Australia is prepared still to defy the appeal of the whole civilized world?" Hughes then pretended not to have heard Wilson, who had to repeat his little speech. Hughes replied, "That's about the size of it, President Wilson."

In the end, Australia gained control of New Guinea. Wilson knew his choices were few: he was not going to war with Australia, obviously, and his economic responses were limited if he chose to use them. Australia did most of its trade with other British possessions and the mother country itself, which was still the richest on Earth, so American economic sanctions would have limited effect and only anger the Australians and the British

Funnily enough, and though they weren't asked, the tribes of New Guinea generally preferred the Germans to the Aussies. The Germans essentially let the tribesmen be, as they did not interfere with the practice of head-hunting (as long as the victim wasn't German) or send missionaries into tribal areas. As long as the Germans could get crops, like palm oil, and use the ports, they were happy. The Australians had been on the island since the start of World War I. They drank to excess, harassed the locals, forbade head-hunting (it went on anyway), and sent missionaries into the jungle, which was not a popular move.

New Zealand was also a Dominion that wanted territory. Considering its small size, New Zealand had sent a large contingent to fight in Europe, and for its trouble, it wanted German Samoa. They, too, engaged in a war of words with Wilson but nothing as dramatic as Hughes's great retort. In the end, New Zealand gained control of the islands.

South Africa

When people think of the end of World War I, they frequently think of Woodrow Wilson's Fourteen Points and the League of Nations, another Wilsonian idea. But what most don't know is that after Wilson announced his Fourteen Points and mentioned a "general association of nations" in a speech to Congress in January 1918, he didn't flesh them out in any real way until he got to Paris.

The other Allied leaders heard the speech, and realizing its importance, they rushed to develop some ideas of their own before they might have something simply foisted upon them by Wilson when they met. The British set up an extensive committee, and the French, who were not as impressed by Wilson's idealism and were determined to go their own way as much as possible after the bloodbath they experienced, set up a small group.

One other man took it upon himself to flesh out Wilson's ideas. This was Field Marshal Jan Smuts of South Africa, which was another Dominion of the United Kingdom. Smuts, who was to play a major advisory role in World War II as well, was a brilliant man. He had literally captured Winston Churchill in the Boer War between the British and Dutch South Africans in 1899 (they later became fast friends). Smuts, the preeminent figure of South African politics, was the commander of the British forces in East Africa in World War I and then made a member of the British Imperial War Cabinet.

Smuts developed a plan for a strong League of Nations, which Wilson came to like and appropriated much from when he fashioned his own more concrete plan. Smuts also tried to incorporate Wilson's idealistic Fourteen Points into the Paris peace talks and the Treaty of Versailles, with various levels of success.

However, despite the sentiments of the League of Nations and the Fourteen Points, Smuts still wanted territory for the Union of South Africa, his country's official name. The territory he wanted was today's Namibia, which had been a German colony for years. In the end, Smuts and South Africa became the "mandatory power" that essentially held control of Namibia until 1990.

Belgium

The Treaty of Versailles was not just one document, though on June 28th, 1919, which was the fifth anniversary of the assassination of Austrian Archduke Franz Ferdinand, the event that began the war, the main document, essentially pertaining to Germany, was signed. No, the talks surrounding the end of World War I and the condition of the world after the war went on for some time and produced a large number of other documents, most of them pertaining to boundaries and armaments.

The men in Paris were essentially trying to remake the world, and their talks encompassed many issues and concerned many lands—too many for this short introductory book. However, one last nation and its post-war desires should be mentioned here: Belgium.

Belgium was invaded by the Germans on their way into France, and most of Belgium remained under German occupation for the whole war. Though the Germans of World War I were angelic compared to the Nazis in World War II, Belgium did not have an easy time of it. Allied propaganda (mainly British and mainly aimed at getting the US involved in the war) did exaggerate German crimes in Belgium, but everyone called the invasion of Belgium the "Rape of Belgium," and it was an appropriate name. Belgium had no part in the competition and hatred between France and Germany. It wanted to remain neutral in any confrontation between the two, but when Germany invaded, it could not. The name given to the German invasion not only reflects Belgium's "innocence" in the rivalry between France and Germany but also the crimes that went on during the occupation—and the sexual assault of Belgian women and girls was definitely a part of that.

Belgium was also, for its size, a rich country. It controlled today's Democratic Republic of the Congo, a huge territory in the heart of south-central Africa. The Congo was rich and strategically placed, and Belgium, aside from its suffering during the occupation, was determined to be treated as a world power, which it was not. (As an aside, it should be remembered that "innocent" Belgium had committed the worst kinds of atrocities in its occupation of the Congo in the 1800s).

Considering that many in England and France used Belgium as a rallying cry in their war effort, it will surprise many that Belgium was essentially ignored at the Paris Peace Conference. It received control of the former German colony of Rwanda, which they held until 1962, a slice of German-controlled territory that remains a part of Belgium today, and a small slice of a German concession in China. Basically, Belgium was told, "Here. Take this. Now go away."

Chapter 5 – The Fourteen Points

Before we go any further, Woodrow Wilson's Fourteen Points needs to be examined, as any discussion of the Treaty of Versailles and how it came about needs to include it. The Fourteen Points formed a base from which the Treaty of Versailles could be built on, or so Wilson and many Americans thought. Because of what followed and the nature of the end product of the Paris Peace Conference (the Treaty of Versailles), the Fourteen Points have gotten a bad reputation. They are looked upon as a "pie in the sky" idealistic dream of a man whose real experience in the world of foreign policy and how the world worked was virtually nil.

People, at the time and since, have also viewed Wilson as a reflection of the opinions of America as a whole, and for the most part, this is true. It should be remembered that when the war broke out, the United States was determined to remain neutral, and the relationship between Great Britain and the US was not as strong as it was after World War I. Americans were suspicious of the UK, and they frowned upon its imperial control of much of the world. After all, the US had once been part of that empire, and what many people called the Second American Revolution (the War of 1812) was not that far in the past. Idealism was part of the American psyche, and not only had the American Revolution been based on those ideals, but so had the Civil War.

America also chafed at Britain's control of much of the world's trade. The US was the rising power, and in the minds of many Americans, they needed Great Britain to "get out of the way." The United States had, by joining the war against imperial and authoritarian Germany, come to the rescue of the Old World, and it was not about to let it return to the behaviors that had gotten them into World War I in the first place.

So, what were the Fourteen Points? Here they are, in their entirety:

> I. Open covenants of peace, openly arrived at, after which there shall be no private international understandings of any kind but diplomacy shall proceed always frankly and in the public view.
>
> II. Absolute freedom of navigation upon the seas, outside territorial waters, alike in peace and in war, except as the seas may be closed in whole or in part by international action for the enforcement of international covenants.
>
> III. The removal, so far as possible, of all economic barriers and the establishment of an equality of trade conditions among all the nations consenting to the peace and associating themselves for its maintenance.
>
> IV. Adequate guarantees given and taken that national armaments will be reduced to the lowest point consistent with domestic safety.
>
> V. A free, open-minded, and absolutely impartial adjustment of all colonial claims, based upon a strict observance of the principle that in determining all such questions of sovereignty the interests of the populations concerned must have equal weight with the equitable claims of the government whose title is to be determined.
>
> VI. The evacuation of all Russian territory and such a settlement of all questions affecting Russia as will secure

the best and freest cooperation of the other nations of the world in obtaining for her an unhampered and unembarrassed opportunity for the independent determination of her own political development and national policy and assure her of a sincere welcome into the society of free nations under institutions of her own choosing; and, more than a welcome, assistance also of every kind that she may need and may herself desire. The treatment accorded Russia by her sister nations in the months to come will be the acid test of their good will, of their comprehension of her needs as distinguished from their own interests, and of their intelligent and unselfish sympathy.

VII. Belgium, the whole world will agree, must be evacuated and restored, without any attempt to limit the sovereignty which she enjoys in common with all other free nations. No other single act will serve as this will serve to restore confidence among the nations in the laws which they have themselves set and determined for the government of their relations with one another. Without this healing act the whole structure and validity of international law is forever impaired.

VIII. All French territory should be freed and the invaded portions restored, and the wrong done to France by Prussia in 1871 in the matter of Alsace-Lorraine, which has unsettled the peace of the world for nearly fifty years, should be righted, in order that peace may once more be made secure in the interest of all.

IX. A readjustment of the frontiers of Italy should be effected along clearly recognizable lines of nationality.

X. The peoples of Austria-Hungary, whose place among the nations we wish to see safeguarded and assured, should be accorded the freest opportunity to autonomous development.

XI. Romania, Serbia, and Montenegro should be evacuated; occupied territories restored; Serbia accorded free and secure access to the sea; and the relations of the several Balkan states to one another determined by friendly counsel along historically established lines of allegiance and nationality; and international guarantees of the political and economic independence and territorial integrity of the several Balkan states should be entered into.

XII. The Turkish portion of the present Ottoman Empire should be assured a secure sovereignty, but the other nationalities which are now under Turkish rule should be assured an undoubted security of life and an absolutely unmolested opportunity of autonomous development, and the Dardanelles should be permanently opened as a free passage to the ships and commerce of all nations under international guarantees.

XIII. An independent Polish state should be erected which should include the territories inhabited by indisputably Polish populations, which should be assured a free and secure access to the sea, and whose political and economic independence and territorial integrity should be guaranteed by international covenant.

XIV. A general association of nations must be formed under specific covenants for the purpose of affording mutual guarantees of political independence and territorial integrity to great and small states alike.

The Fourteen Points became the basis of the Paris Peace Conference for a variety of reasons. The French and the British, other than wanting to punish Germany (though they differed, as France wanted a more severe treaty) and carve up slices of its empire, did not truly have a comprehensive plan to end the war and establish peace. Remember, the Germans did not surrender, at least officially; they simply approached Wilson for a truce. Unfortunately for the Germans, they were in no position to resist if the terms of the final treaty were unacceptable, which turned out to be the case.

In the time since World War I, Wilson's plan has been the subject of intense scrutiny. Would the Fourteen Points have been better achieved if the victorious European powers had not been so eager to alter them in their favor or ignore them? Was Wilson's plan too idealistic? Too general? Nonetheless, the Fourteen Points was the only concrete plan put forward whose aim was to construct not just an end to the war but a plan for maintaining peace. It was also a clear statement of American ideals. Wilson and the United States had been under great pressure to join the Allies from the day the war started. Wilson and most Americans in government and outside of it remembered George Washington's appeal to future generations in his Farewell Address to not involve themselves in European wars and their alliances, which so often dragged nations into war against their better interests. Until World War I, Washington's appeal was almost literally "gospel" for American politicians.

In 1914 and until America's entry into the war, the majority of Americans believed the US should keep out of the conflict. Many of them harbored a great disdain for anything European at all, though most believed that Germany, Austria-Hungary, and the Ottoman Empire were the aggressors.

However, there were sizable portions of the US population that wished to see America enter the war on the Allied side. The Allies represented democracy; Britain, after all, was the country with whom the US shared much of its culture and, of course, its language,

France had helped the United States during the American Revolution, and millions of Italians were coming to the US at the start of the 20th century, joining those who were already there.

On the other hand, there were millions of German Americans and a sizable portion from the nationalities that made up the Austro-Hungarian Empire; however, the number of Turkish immigrants to the US was small and remains so today. And lastly, there were the Irish Americans, many of whom had been in the country for centuries and others who began coming in waves in the 1840s due to the great Potato Famine, which killed hundreds of thousands of people. As such, most of the Irish Americans had no love for Great Britain and the English, who had held Ireland as a colony for hundreds of years.

When the US entered the war as a result of German missteps and very successful British propaganda, Wilson was determined that it would be a one-time thing and that America, as the new rising power in the world, would use all the power at its command, both actual and potential, to ensure that the United States was not dragged into another European war. Going further, Wilson intended his Fourteen Points (and its League of Nations) to be the basis of ending war—for all time.

Each of the Fourteen Points touched upon an issue that Wilson and many others felt had been responsible for starting or contributing to the start of the war or prolonging it.

The first point, summarized as "open covenants, openly arrived at," reflects Wilson's and America's concern that for too long, the great European powers had dealt with each other secretly, dividing up the spoils of war in a way that would only bring on more problems or cause more wars. This also tied into a later point, number five, regarding "colonial claims," which has become more familiarly known as "self-determination of peoples." By openly arriving at agreements with no secret clauses, it was hoped that, among other things, the many minorities in the world would see that the great powers were working to recognize their needs.

Point two, regarding "freedom of the seas," was tied into point three, which dealt with the "freedom of trade." For too long, the European powers had dominated the seas and restricted trade when and where they wished, and though it was not mentioned openly, this point was quite clearly aimed at Great Britain, who still, in 1919, had the most powerful navy and trading fleet in the world.

The fourth point, which dealt with armaments, seemed quite obvious to everyone after the war. If nations only kept enough weapons and men to defend themselves, wars would never start. This is likely the most idealistic of Wilson's Fourteen Points, and while we may laugh at it today, it was highly popular in a time when pacifism as a political force was powerful, as people wished to avoid a repeat of the losses of World War I in the future.

Point five, along with the terms given to Germany in the Treaty of Versailles, was the main problem. The idea behind point five is that people (meaning groups of people, usually defined as ethnicities but also as people wishing to unite behind a political cause as well) had the right to their independence, meaning no more colonies or empires. We're going to come back to point five later on because the issues brought up in this point were instrumental for the future of the world.

Points six through thirteen dealt with problems and boundaries in Russia, Poland, and the former Austro-Hungarian and Ottoman Empires. These points went hand in hand with point five, as the issues of how the borders of these territories/former empires were going to have a direct effect on the post-WWI world and the beginning of WWII.

Lastly, the fourteenth point called for what became known as the League of Nations, which Wilson envisioned as an organization of governments around the world in which nations could peacefully air out their grievances and hopefully come up with solutions to their issues. Georges Clemenceau summed up the feeling of many, especially the larger powers of the world, when he said, "I like the League, but I don't believe in it," meaning that it was a great idea but that it would likely never work. Many Europeans felt the same way—they wanted a different way to deal with each other but were skeptical that it would ever happen. Smaller powers, and nations yet to be, such as Poland, loved the League, at least at first, because it gave them an opportunity to present their cases to the rest of the world without the threat of war.

What Wilson did not realize, or what he chose to ignore, was that the League had no real power to enforce its decisions unless the nations of the world chose to do so. Though some proposed an "international police force" or an "army of peacekeepers," these plans never really got off the drawing board. In the end, nations would behave as people behaved. If it was in their best interest to use force, and the odds of them being victorious were high enough, then nations would use force, especially if there were no consequences.

Still, despite all of its glaring weaknesses and the fact that no one at the time of the Paris Peace Conference had a real idea of what its structure would be like, Wilson held on to the League as the most important of his plan and the one thing he most wanted in the final agreements of the Paris Peace Conference.

Woodrow Wilson was a student of history. In some ways, he was not a very good student, but he did know American political history. For instance, the Founding Fathers of the United States had deliberately kept the US Constitution vague in many spots in order to keep it flexible with the passage of time and to allow the states to keep certain powers to themselves. Wilson, when asked about the lack of structure for the League in his ideas, speeches, and articles, often responded in terms that gave the impression that he had intentionally left the structure rather vague. Nations could hammer these out in the League itself, and besides, how was he, or anyone else, to know what problems might arise in the future—like the Founding Fathers thought, that was better left to the generations to come.

Perhaps Wilson's vagueness was intentional, or perhaps he was just covering for his own lack of specific ideas, but if the League was to be the one thing that Wilson insisted be in the final treaty, he did one thing to ensure that it was doomed to fail: he made sure, by his arrogance, that the United States would never be a member of the League of Nations.

As we mentioned earlier, Wilson's entourage did not include his opposition, the Republicans. Of course, the Republicans wanted to be included in Wilson's entourage. In a democracy, the opposition should at least have a voice in national affairs, but Wilson had completely shut them out. He did not want to have anyone gainsay his ideas, especially publicly, while he was in Paris. This was Wilson's moment, and he was not going to share it with anyone.

Perhaps Wilson believed that his job would be made more difficult if he had to negotiate with the Republicans while he was in Paris, but he was going to have to negotiate with them at some point. Even if he returned from France with the perfect treaty, the Republicans, with their own political interests, were going to have to oppose him on some things. By not including them at all, Wilson made sure that they were going to oppose him on virtually everything. Additionally, conservative Democrats, especially from Irish and German constituencies, were bound to oppose him as well. Wilson opposed even small changes, even though the Republicans accepted the general idea of the League of Nations and the Treaty of Versailles.

Many people around the world knew that the United States was *the* rising power, and that without it, the League was likely doomed to fail.

Chapter 6 – The Scrambled Map and People of Europe

If you're European, what follows will likely be common knowledge, but for many Americans not familiar with the map and people of Europe, it might come as a surprise to learn that within many of the nations of Europe, there are many minorities with different cultures, backgrounds, and languages.

For example, take Belgium. Belgium itself is made up primarily of two ethnic groups, the Flemish, who live mainly in the north of the country and who speak Dutch, and the Walloons, who live in the south and speak French. Even since World War II, there have been times where large portions of each of these populations have wanted their own nation. Adding to that, in the southeastern part of the country, which encompasses the Ardennes Forest of World War II fame, many of the people speak German, and laws have recently been passed allowing schools in that part of the country to teach in German.

In Scandinavia, the border areas of Sweden and Finland have mixed populations. In some areas of Sweden, many people speak Finnish, and vice versa. Throughout Scandinavia, the Sámi people (formerly known to many as "Lapps") are a completely distinct group of people with a unique language and who, until very recently, made their living from reindeer herding.

When you get to Eastern Europe and the western part of Russia and Ukraine, the situation gets even more confusing. Because of wars, politics, economies, cultures, geography, and much else, the ethnic groups of Eastern Europe were (and to some extent still are) all mixed together.

In Ukraine today, a war is being fought between ethnic Russians and Ukrainians over the eastern part of that country. In the Baltic states of Lithuania, Latvia, and especially Estonia, Russians are a sizable minority, and many of them feel persecuted. Czechoslovakia, which was formed after World War I, split in 1993 because of disagreements between the Czechs and the Slovaks. In northern Spain and southern France, the Basque people, who many geneticists believe to be the first distinct European people, are minorities, and until recently, they participated in a low-level guerrilla struggle for more autonomy and independence, especially in Spain. The Catalans of Spain recently protested for more autonomy, with the protests being put down. And this just describes Europe today. Imagine what it was like in 1918, 1919, and 1920 after World War I and the Russian Revolution. Imagine how bloody and violent it was, especially since values at the time were a bit different and news media was much more primitive, restricting information and images.

One of the new nations to come out of World War I was Poland. Since the mid/late 1700s, what we know as Poland (albeit with different borders) was divided between Prussia, Austria-Hungary, and Russia. At one point before that, Poland was a large empire. In concert with then-powerful Lithuania, it controlled the Baltic states and much of western Russia and Ukraine. Within that area alone, ethnic rivalries (a polite way of saying "hatred") were strong, as each group had a history of oppressing the other. From 1919 to 1920, Poland reformed as a nation, and one of the things that the new Poland did right away was invade Russia and Ukraine in an attempt to seize as much territory for itself as possible before the Treaty of Versailles and its subsidiary treaties made this much more difficult.

When the Bolsheviks came to power, they signed the Treaty of Brest-Litovsk with the Germans, which gave Germany all of Ukraine and a huge chunk of western Russia. Many people point to this draconian treaty that Germany forced on Russia as an excuse for the Treaty of Versailles. What's important here is that when Germany was defeated, a power vacuum existed in those areas, and Poland rushed to fill it, and they did so until 1922 when they were thrown out by the resurgent Soviet Union.

The whole episode was one filled with violence of the most brutal kind. Neighbor turned on neighbor in unbelievably savage ways, almost as if they were enacting "revenge" for years of interchangeable oppression, real and imagined.

This is only one example of what Wilson was trying to avoid with his Fourteen Points. Similar problems went on in Czechoslovakia, Hungary, Romania, Bulgaria, Greece, and Yugoslavia (itself a new country at the time). To his credit, Wilson and the men of the Paris Peace Conference tried to deal with these problems as best they could. It was not easy, and it did not please everyone, but there is likely no way it could have.

Out of the Austro-Hungarian Empire came a slew of new nations, like Czechoslovakia, Hungary, and Yugoslavia.

In Czechoslovakia, a successful parliamentary democracy arose, and for a time, the ethnic rivalries between the two major groups were put aside, at least to a degree. However, a third group would become one of the thorniest problems they faced in the late 1930s. This was the sizable German-speaking minority in the far northwest of Czechoslovakia, the Sudeten Germans, named for the Sudeten Mountains where many of them lived.

Having been the dominant group for centuries, the Germans in what became Czechoslovakia were now on the bottom. Old resentments returned, and among other things, the German language was suppressed, at least in schools and in politics and the media. In turn, more resentments were made.

The Hungarians had had substantial autonomy under the Austrian Habsburg ruling family, but they chafed for many years for their own nation or kingdom. After World War I, this became a reality, although it came with some major and unpleasant changes if you were Hungarian. In the area between Hungary and Romania, the populations were relatively intertwined: the Hungarians lived in majority Romanian areas and vice versa. The Hungarians living in Romania were discriminated against to an extent, and so were the Romanians, but the worst excesses were prevented, at least within the Habsburg (Austro-Hungarian) Empire, as they were suppressed by laws and the police.

When World War I ended, the major powers of the Paris Peace Conference moved the borders of Romania and Hungary. This was partially meant to be a "punishment" against the Hungarians and partly to address the grievances of the (former) Romanian minority in the area. Romania grew in size, while Hungary shrank—and not just a little—and many Hungarians now found themselves living in Romania.

The territory of Alsace-Lorraine was returned to France, but as many people at the time recognized, most of the people living there did not want to be French. To a degree, Clemenceau and the French press were right: most of the ethnic French had been driven out of the area during the war. The people remaining were German, and, of course, they would want to belong to Germany. "But," said Clemenceau and every other Frenchman and woman, "it was France." In 1940, Hitler would reannex the area to Germany. When World War II ended, France took it back, and it still remains French today, with very few Germans in it.

As can be seen, the Austro-Hungarian Empire had disintegrated in the last days of the war. The empire had fought against the Russians, the Serbs, the Italians, and the Romanians. Casualties were high, and the unity of the kingdom, already fragile at the start of the war, came apart by the fall of 1918. Since that time, the people who populated the empire attempted to establish their own governments and their own boundaries. By the time of the Paris Peace Conference in 1919, the boundaries of what was to become Yugoslavia were already completely set, which was one reason why the Italians did not get the territory on the western side of the Adriatic that they wanted.

Unfortunately, for the many people that made up Yugoslavia, the dominant power was Serbia. This is not the place to retrace the beginning of World War I, but let's take a moment to briefly outline it because Serbia and the Austro-Hungarian Empire is where it began.

In 1914, Serbia was an independent landlocked kingdom. Like many other European nations at the time, one of its main interests was gaining more territory. Unfortunately for Serbia, its largest and nearest neighbor was a world power, Austria-Hungary.

Many Serbs within the government, and especially in the military, had an idea that all Slavic peoples living in the Balkans should be united under the Serbian flag. "Yugoslavia" literally means "Land of the South Slavs," and it included Croats, Bosnians, Montenegrins, and Slovenes. Other smaller groups, such as the Albanians and Slavic Macedonians, were there as well.

The Austro-Hungarians resented the "hole" in their empire—Serbia—and they also had a tenuous grasp on the other groups mentioned above. To them, Serbia was a nuisance, and the Austro-Hungarian military meant to deal with it. They just needed an excuse, which a secret group within the Serbian military provided.

The Black Hand, as this secretive group called itself, found three willing and not too bright Serbian nationalists to carry out the assassination of Austrian Archduke Franz Ferdinand. When he, along with his wife Sophie, was killed on June 28th, 1914, the series of events that led to World War I was set in motion. Notice that Germany is not mentioned in any of those paragraphs above.

During the war, Croats and Bosnians fought in the Austro-Hungarian Army, while the Serbs fought against it. Many Croats and Bosnians, as well as other ethnic groups, did not want to fight for Austria, but many of them also did not want to be dominated by the

Serbs, whom they hated, mostly (but not exclusively) for reasons of religion. The Serbs were Eastern Orthodox, while the Croats were Catholic and many Bosnians Muslim. There was no love lost between the Croats and the Bosnian Muslims, either. Another ethnic group, the Albanians, occupied a region called Kosovo, which the Serbs believed was their ancestral homeland. To put it simply, the Serbs hated the Kosovar Albanians, just as the Albanians despised the Serbs. On the map below, you can see the religious and ethnic mix of the Balkans (including Greece) in the years before World War I.

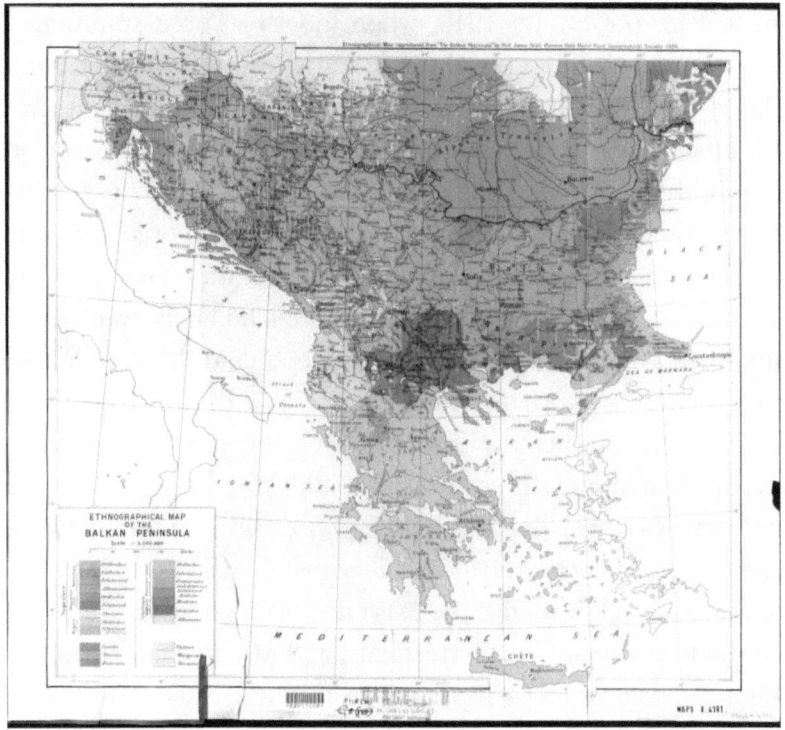

As you can see, there was a reason why many diplomats and politicians called the Balkan Peninsula a "powder keg" and were convinced a general European war would begin there, which it obviously did. In the northwest was the Habsburg (Austro-Hungarian) Empire. In the northeast was Russia, and in the southeast, and at times occupying the region, was the Muslim Ottoman Empire. For centuries, the Balkans had been a battlefield, and the hate ran very, very deep.

Still, despite all the animosity, many people believed that if the ethnicities of what became Yugoslavia could be united under one government, there might be a chance for a lasting peace. Additionally, if these nations were united, rather than existing as separate weak entities, they might be better able to protect themselves from their powerful neighbors, whoever they might turn out to be.

Sadly, for the Croats and other groups, many of whom wanted a more representative government, the Serbians dominated the region. They had an existing army and government, and that was enough for them to take power. By 1919, when the Big Three summoned the groups of Yugoslavia to see them in Paris (they had been waiting for weeks, all the while deciding to form their own government since no one seemed to be interested in helping them), Yugoslavia was a new country with the Serbian king, Peter I, as the head of government.

By the time Wilson, Clemenceau, and Lloyd George agreed to see them, the only question remaining was not whether Yugoslavia should be a country but where its borders should be. Italy wanted a large chunk of coastal land, as we have mentioned, and this was denied, for it was deemed as too obviously "imperial." Imperialism was okay outside of Europe but not inside it. Besides, the Slavs had already made up their minds to go to war should Italy be given any land in "their" territory. So, the Big Three, who were supposed to be the arbiters of the peace and the settlers of all matters within Europe, were forced to acknowledge the existence of Yugoslavia.

At the time, most Croats, Bosnians, and other smaller groups were under no illusions about how they might be treated within the new kingdom. As related in the great 2001 book, *Paris 1919: Six Months That Changed the World* by Margaret MacMillan, the top Croatian diplomat to the conference, Ante Trumbić, was conversing with a Serbian diplomat regarding how the Muslims of Bosnia would be incorporated into the new country. The Serbian diplomat replied that the Muslims would be given 24 to 48 hours to convert to Orthodoxy (remember, the Croats, including Trumbić, were Catholic) or "Those who won't, will be killed, as we have done in our time in Serbia."

Trumbić replied, "You can't be serious," to which the Serbian diplomat answered, "Quite serious."

Luckily for those at the time, neither forcible conversions nor genocide happened. In the 1990s, though, it did. Throughout much of the 1990s, the area of Europe that is formerly known as Yugoslavia was embroiled in a genocidal conflict. That conflict, while the result of age-old unresolved hatred, can also be blamed on what the men in Paris did, or rather didn't, do.

Lastly, the borders between Germany and Poland were moved, and sizable populations shifted in and out. On the next page, you will see a map that illustrates the changes in the borders of Europe as a result of the Paris Peace Conference, the Treaty of Versailles, and the end of World War I.

Chapter 7 – The Middle East

If you look at the bottom left corner of the map above, you will notice that the area labeled "Ottoman Empire" in the top picture is labeled "Turkey" on the bottom. Below Turkey are two new areas—these eventually became the countries of Jordan and Syria, though, in 1919/1920, the great powers decided that these areas and the people within them should become "mandates," which for all intents and purposes means "colonies." So much for "self-determination of peoples."

In today's world, if an American or European politician announced that they believed in "self-determination of peoples" and then followed it with the words "except in the cases of," their career would likely be over. When Wilson made his Fourteen Points speech and then his comments afterward, that's essentially what he did. Like many of the white ruling class of the time, Wilson (and Lloyd George, Clemenceau, and Orlando, among many others) believed that many of the non-white peoples of the world were not capable of self-government. That's one of the reasons it was so "easy" for Europeans to take over so much of the world as colonies.

It must be said that Wilson probably honestly believed what he so often said, that, eventually, most of these people would be capable of self-government, and it would only be at that time that they should receive their independence. Of course, he didn't say what "capable" and "independent" meant.

For the other two great powers of the Big Three, Wilson's "self-determination" was just a phrase that, for the sake of public opinion and to mollify the Americans, they had to seem to agree to. However, they were very mute in their enthusiasm and very careful in choosing their words when asked about it. One look at the map of the world will tell you why.

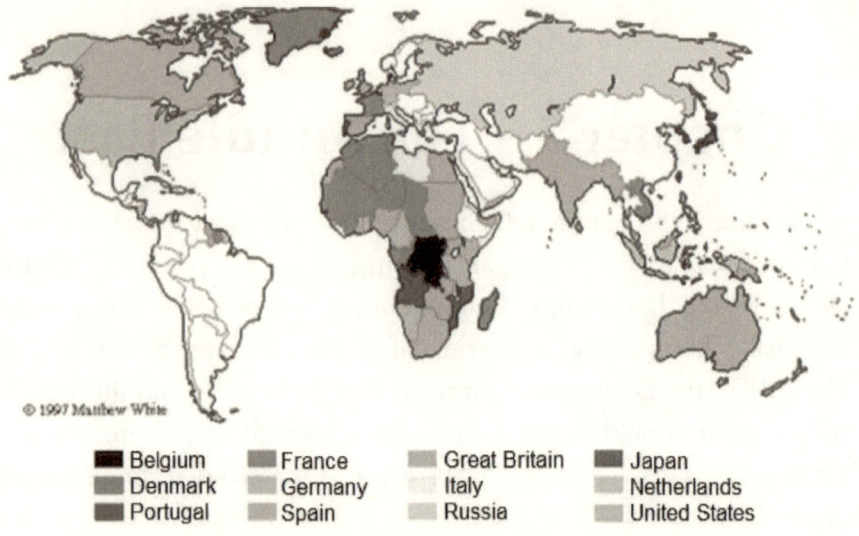

Illustration 6: Colonial possessions in late 1800s/early 1900s. Courtesy Matthew White

The colonial possessions of Britain and France alone spanned much of the world. For the British, its colonial possessions were a matter of survival due to its growing population and an economy reliant on raw materials gotten cheaply. For France, especially after the war and the toll it took on the nation's economy, its colonies were more important than ever. It should also not be forgotten that, at the time, colonial possessions were a mark of a nation's prestige and power, and France and Britain, though allies in the war, had not always been the best of friends.

You might notice on the map the white-filled territories. In the case of China and the countries of Latin America, that indicates independence (though China had to give up portions of its land as "concessions" ever since the 1840s). You'll also notice that Ethiopia in Eastern Africa and Liberia in Western Africa are white, as they were independent nations, along with Persia and Afghanistan. However, the areas of the Middle East were not independent, as the map might seem to indicate. That area, today's Saudi Arabia, Jordan, Israel/Palestine, and Lebanon, was under the control of the Ottoman Turks, as was much of Greece (in which some areas had won independence in the 1830s).

When World War I ended, the Ottoman Empire ceased to be, officially dissolving in 1923. Internal strife, defeat on the battlefields, and guerrilla wars in its territories all contributed to its fall. Britain and France were keen to rush into the vacuum created by the fall of the once-mighty Ottomans. These former Ottoman territories had rapidly become more important at the start of the 20th century, and you can probably guess why—oil. By 1919, the world and its armed forces were powered by oil, and the British and French wanted it for themselves.

In 1919, the Middle East was almost as scrambled ethnographically as Europe. Though, in general, large communities of one or two particular peoples with their own cultures existed, there were many ethnic groups scattered throughout the former Ottoman Empire.

This was particularly true in Turkey, where the western coastal areas were dominated by the Greeks, and the eastern parts were full of Armenians, Georgians, and other groups. Constantinople, its capital, may have been the most ethnically diverse city on the planet. Turks, Greeks, Arabs of all kinds, Jews, Armenians, Bulgarians...the list goes on for quite a while. Any attempt to divide the fallen Ottoman Empire along ethnic lines was a challenge, to say the least.

But the Allies tried. The most famous agreement between the Allies was the 1916 Sykes-Picot Agreement, which was named for the British and French diplomats who helped hammer it out. This agreement was a secret protocol between the British and French, but the Italians and Russians (the other Allies) were privy to it and a part of it as well. Each of these nations, according to the agreement, was to receive, either as colonies or as additions to their nation (especially as far as Russia was concerned), large chunks of the Middle East.

The problem with that was that after the Bolshevik Revolution of 1917, communist leader Leon Trotsky made the agreement public. Of course, this outraged the various peoples of the area, who, after centuries of Ottoman rule, wished independence of some sort for themselves, and it also outraged President Woodrow Wilson, who at the time was formulating his Fourteen Points. Wilson's first point was a direct response to the publication of the Sykes-Picot Agreement. In his mind, and in the mind of many Americans, the Europeans were "at it again," once again dividing up the world between themselves with no thought of the people living there.

There were a number of factors at play in the former Ottoman Empire in 1919. Firstly, in 1908, a group of young Turkish military officers had essentially seized power from the Ottoman sultan, who, truth be told, was ill-equipped to rule and was relieved in a way to not have to anymore. These men are known to history as the Young Turks, and they led Turkey to disaster.

For centuries, the Ottoman Empire practiced a kind of tolerance that was rare in many parts of the world. Islam was the state religion, but Christians, Jews, and other minority religions were allowed to worship in relative peace. They paid higher taxes and had to recognize Islam as the state religion, but for the most part, they were left alone. The Greeks dominated trade in the west, the Armenians were advisers to the sultan, and many non-Turks served in the military.

The Young Turks believed that Turks were becoming second-class citizens in their own empire, and so, they began a systematic pogrom of discrimination. This reached its height in the Armenian Genocide, which took place between 1915 and 1923, in which an estimated one million or more Armenians were killed, starved to death, died of disease or famine, or were dispersed from their traditional lands.

Other ethnic groups saw this and feared they could be next, and during World War I, there were massive uprisings against Turkish rule, especially in the lands of today's Saudi Arabia. This was made famous in the film *Lawrence of Arabia* (1962), which depicts British officer T.E Lawrence helping to lead an Arab revolt against the Turks.

When World War I ended and the men of Paris got together, they each had differing plans. One man who has not been mentioned yet is Greek Prime Minister Eleutherios Venizelos. At the end of the war, Venizelos pressed the Big Three for territory in western Turkey that he believed had been traditionally Greek. In a way, he was right, but he had to go back to the time of the Byzantine Empire and ancient Greece to prove it. Still, the Greeks were a sizable population in western Turkey, and it seemed only natural that the Greeks controlled Turkish Thrace, the part of Turkey that lies in Europe. But this was not enough for the Greeks, and so, they marched into western/central Turkey. From 1919 to 1922, the Turks and Greeks fought a completely savage war that saw not only the defeat of Greece but also the removal of all Turks from Greece and all Greeks from Turkey. It also saw the rise of what many in Turkey believe is the greatest Turk of them all, Mustafa Kemal, who was known as "Kemal Atatürk," meaning, "Kemal, father of the Turks." Atatürk had led the Ottomans to victory over the British Imperial Force during the naval campaigns in the Dardanelles during World War I, which took place between 1915 and 1916. After the defeat of the Greeks in 1922, he centralized power in Turkey and established a surprisingly modern dictatorship with the goal of bringing Turkey into the 20th century.

The Greco-Turkish War was not the only war in which blood was being spilled. Throughout the Middle East, different peoples were waging low-level civil wars against each other, much of it based around religion.

In the late 1800s, Zionism became a rallying cry among Jews in Europe and throughout the world. In a nutshell, Zionism called for the return of Jews to Palestine (as it was known then) and the formation of the state of Israel. By 1919, thousands of Jews had made the trip to the area. Communities of Jews settled in various areas and were mostly self-governing. The problem was, though, that they were surrounded by mostly hostile Muslim Arab tribes. In other areas, Arab Christians, which were a sizable minority, especially in Lebanon, also felt under threat.

Both Lloyd George and Wilson were exceedingly religious. They realized that without protection, the religious minorities in the Middle East might be eliminated or, at the very least, driven out. For this reason, and for reasons involving oil and to block any move by the new Soviet Union into the Middle East, it was agreed that the area would be divided into mandates. Those areas would be like colonies, but they would be given (in some cases) some autonomy of rule or a guarantee that at some future date, they would be given their own country.

The United States, at this time, was more than self-sufficient when it came to oil, and the nation was already involved in governing the Philippines and Puerto Rico, as well as being occupied with issues in Central America; thus, the US government did not support their country getting involved in the Middle East. The European powers would have to take care of the Middle East on their own—not that they minded.

Though it took some time to come to final agreements, the borders of the Middle East ended up looking as they do in the excellent map below.

Illustration 7: Additionally, Egypt was and had been a British protectorate, with some autonomy for the Egyptians. Libya had been Italian since 1911, and Algeria, Tunisia, and part of Morocco was French before the war. Spain controlled the other part of Morocco.

In the United States, both Wilson's allies and his opponents saw this as a betrayal of his Fourteen Points, and they believed that he had been duped by the Europeans, who were simply doing what they had done for centuries. As the years went by, more and more Americans came to see the US involvement in World War I as a lie—to them, it was clear the Europeans had no intention of changing their behavior. So, many Americans determined that if (or rather "when") the Europeans asked for help, America would mind its own business and leave Europe to fight its own battles. This was one of the major reasons for the strength of the isolationist movement of the late 1930s and early 1940s.

Chapter 8 – Germany

To understand what happened to Germany at the end of World War I and beyond into the 1930s, we have to discuss not only Germany's defeat but also how Germany got involved in the war. As you may know, even if you've only read the small mentions of it in this book, Germany was blamed for starting World War I by the British, French, and, tacitly, the United States.

Within the actual Treaty of Versailles, this is called the War Guilt Clause. Officially, this is Article 231 of the Treaty of Versailles, and it went: The Allied and Associated Governments affirm and Germany accepts the responsibility of Germany and her allies for causing *all* [author's italics] the loss and damage to which the Allied and Associated Governments and their nationals have been subjected as a consequence of the war imposed upon them by the aggression of Germany and her allies.

You can see that Germany is the only country listed by name in the clause. There are two reasons for that. The first is clear—Germany was being called out by name, placing the blame on the Germans alone. Germany's main allies, Austria-Hungary and the Ottoman Empire, didn't exist any longer (or wouldn't exist much longer in the case of the Ottoman Empire), but the clause could have read "Germany and its allies, the former Austro-Hungarian and Ottoman Empires" or something similar. Germany's final ally, Bulgaria, wasn't even mentioned, as it was too minor and too poor to really matter. And then there is that little word — "all." The omission of those three letters might have altered history, at least to a degree.

There are many reasons for this. Germany was the most powerful of the Central Powers and had inflicted significantly more damage on the Allies than the other three. It was also the richest. Historically (for France anyway), Germany had been the problem, and the Allies meant to deal with it for once and for all.

In the eyes of most Germans, however, Germany had not started the war. That honor could be laid at the feet of the Austro-Hungarians or the Serbians. Germany was only doing what any other nation in the world would have done, backing its ally. This simple answer is true, to an extent. But like most international matters, the start of the war is a bit more complicated than that.

You've already read how militants with the Serbian military and population contrived to assassinate Austrian Archduke Franz Ferdinand in Sarajevo, Bosnia, in June 1914. The archduke and his wife were there to visit the provinces and to show the Bosnians and others in the Balkans (notably the Serbs) that Austria was still highly involved in the politics of the area and would assert its control when needed. The Serbs involved with the Black Hand hoped that the assassination of the archduke would cause reasonable Austrians to see that the Balkans were violent and ungovernable and that they would hopefully decide it was best to leave them be. In that case, the Serbians could fulfill a long-held dream of uniting the South Slavs in one kingdom under a Serbian king.

Of course, it did not happen like that. Any reasonable person could have predicted what the Austrian reaction was going to be. The Serbians killed the heir to the Austro-Hungarian throne (he wasn't very popular in Austria, but that didn't matter). Already seen as one of the "weak men of Europe," the Austrians could not afford to do nothing, so they delivered the Serbians an ultimatum, a list of demands that the Serbians must follow if they wished to avoid a war.

More importantly, the Austrian Emperor Franz Josef I contacted his most powerful ally, German Kaiser Wilhelm II, before the delivery of this ultimatum. In response, Wilhelm gave Franz Josef what is infamously known as the "blank check." Basically, Germany would go along with anything the Austro-Hungarians decided to do, and they would support them no matter what the consequences might be.

Wilhelm II knew full well what the consequences might be—an all-European war. Austria's demands on Serbia were so over the top that no country could agree to them and retain its independence. Among them were giving the Austrian police carte-blanche within Serbia to conduct a search for any conspirators and the suppression of any anti-Austrian newspaper articles or books. And that was just two of the items in the ultimatum. There was no way the Serbians could agree.

So, what did the Serbians do? They contacted their "big brother," Russia, which was allied with France and Great Britain. Tsar Nicholas II assured the Serbs that should the Austro-Hungarians invade, Russia would mobilize its huge army and intervene. That being the case, the Serbs told Austria-Hungary to "get lost." This set off a chain reaction of troop mobilizations and movements, with each country having been waiting for a general war for at least a generation. Though there were many other factors contributing to the start of the war, including personal rivalries between some of the crowned heads of Europe, that is how the war began.

As far as the Central Powers were concerned, though, Germany was the last man standing, as well as the richest man standing.

The problem was Germany was only rich in potential, not cash or gold reserves. Those were long gone due to the expenditures made during the war. But even if Germany was bankrupt in 1918/19, the country itself had not been invaded, and its infrastructure and businesses were still intact. Germany's population in 1920 was 61 million, which was down four million from casualties and the loss of

Alsace-Lorraine, but it was still significantly higher than every other European country. Besides that, its workforce was known to be one of the best and most hard-working in the world. So, the Allies would have to come up with a plan to make sure that Germany paid for what it had done. This came in the form of "reparations" and outright payments from any reserve treasure Germany held and from its industrious workforce.

But there were many problems surrounding Germany in regards to its ability and willingness to pay, some of which have already been briefly touched on. To start off, the German population was under the belief, at least until just before the end, that the war was going well or, at the very least, okay. German troops were still occupying parts of France and all of Belgium, and no foreign troops had ever crossed into Germany. The newspapers said the Allies were on their last legs, and though news saying otherwise did get into Germany via troops on leave, foreign newspapers smuggled in, and the nature of life in Germany (tens of thousands of crippled veterans on the streets, and decreasing amounts of food due to the British blockade), many in Germany chose to believe that victory was right around the corner. This is what the generals kept telling them, and generals were among the most esteemed people in Germany, long before World War I.

In the spring of 1918, the Germans were able to mount a huge offensive in France because they had come to an "arrangement" with the Russians, who were now calling their country the Union of Soviet Socialist Republics, also known as the USSR or the Soviet Union. Having overthrown Tsar Nicholas II, the Soviets were embroiled in a conflict with his extended family and conservative elements in the country. The Russian Civil War would be fought from 1918 to 1921, and the Soviets could not wage war against the Germans and the conservatives at the same time.

The Soviet government agreed to the terms of the Treaty of Brest-Litovsk in March 1918, which gave Germany a huge swath of western Russia, all of Ukraine, and the Baltic states. This represented the most resource-rich and industrialized area of the country. For the

Bolsheviks, it was a temporary price that needed to be paid. Once the civil war was won, they could try to win it back, or perhaps Germany would have lost the war (and with the US joining against it, that last scenario seemed likely), and the lost territories would return to the USSR anyway.

When people complained about the harshness of the Treaty of Versailles and how it treated Germany, others pointed to the Treaty of Brest-Litovsk, whose stipulations were much harsher in total than what was signed in Paris. The Treaty of Brest-Litovsk included such terms as greater reparation payments, one-third of all coal production in the former Russian Empire, and one-third of its food production.

With the signing of the Treaty of Brest-Litovsk, the Germans shifted hundreds of thousands of troops to the Western Front in the hopes of defeating the Allies once and for all (or, at the very least, bring them to the peace table) before the Americans could truly join in. When General Ludendorff's Spring Offensive failed, the high command of the German Army knew it was only a matter of time before Germany would have to either surrender and hopefully eke out tolerable peace terms or be completely defeated and invaded.

By the fall of 1918, the German Army was in tatters. Ammunition was short. Supplies were running low. Replacements were fewer and younger, and what there were of them could not be trained properly because bodies were needed at the front immediately. In Germany itself, discontent was mounting, as food riots and labor unrest broke out across the country almost every day. And the Americans were now fighting at the front with a million men, with more on the way, and they were bringing limitless supplies along with them.

On September 29th, 1918, Generals Hindenburg and Ludendorff went to Kaiser Wilhelm II and told him that the war was lost. They suggested that the best course of action would be to approach American President Woodrow Wilson and ask for an armistice based on his proposals announced in the Fourteen Points and other speeches. It took until November for the decision to be made and the armistice to be announced.

By that time, the Kaiser had abdicated his throne. Germany, in theory, had been a parliamentary democracy since its founding in 1871, but the real power lay in the hands of the chancellor, Otto von Bismarck, but after Bismarck was fired by the Kaiser in 1890, that power was in Wilhelm's hands. Parliament (in German, the Reichstag) met and was able to pass laws that the Kaiser agreed with, but the real power lay with Wilhelm, as well as with the military, which, at the beginning of the war, began to increase in power.

In November, when Hindenburg and Ludendorff recommended approaching Wilson, they had it in mind that the leading members of the Reichstag would be the ones to approach the Allies. It couldn't be the military for a variety of reasons. The Allies would be more likely to listen to civilian leaders, and more importantly, if anything went wrong, the military could not be blamed for it.

That last sentence is extremely important in understanding what came next, for two reasons. One is the status of the military in Germany before and during the war. Second is because of the theories that developed in Germany regarding the end of World War I.

Chapter 9 – The "Stab-in-the-Back" Myth

Hitler wasn't the first German to develop the idea that Germany had been betrayed from within, resulting in the humiliations that came with the Treaty of Versailles. Hitler made his first public speech in March 1920, and in that speech, he spoke about "a world of enemies." By that, he referred to the vast international array that marched against Germany during the war: France, Great Britain, and the United States, among others. Hitler did not speak about "internal enemies." That was a theme he developed later when it caught on in the right-wing circles that he had begun to travel in.

The *Dolchstoßlegende* (literally "dagger stab myth"), known in English as "the stab-in-the-back myth," was the implication that enemies from within Germany had stabbed the military and its soldiers "in the back" by fomenting labor unrest, inflation, anti-war legislation (which never passed and never could, given the structure of the German parliament of the time), food hoarding, communist agitation, and sending out peace-feelers to the Allies. Communists, socialists (which are not the same thing, especially in Wilhelmine Germany), pacifists, capitalist money lenders (which was code for "the Jews" and foreign banks), and the Jewish community were all to blame for Germany's defeat. However, what really defeated Germany was the overwhelming arrangement of forces from around the world that opposed it.

During World War I, Hitler's Bavarian regiment, the List Regiment, named after its commander, fought British, French, Australian, Indian, Canadian, New Zealand, South African, and American troops. After the war, veterans (including Hitler) spoke of being demoralized by seeing so much of the world arrayed against Germany. Hitler, in later speeches and writings, spoke of saying to himself, "These lads, blond and blue-eyed, who are they really? They are all former German farmer's sons. Now they are our enemies." This thought was one of the building blocks of Hitler's *Lebensraum* ("living space") ideology, which called for Germany to expand into the "empty" and vast lands of Eastern Europe and Russia. In his mind, Germany would not have lost millions of emigrants to the US, Australia, and Canada, to name but a few countries, if Germany had had the space for its excess population.

As peacetime grew more chaotic and depressing for the Germans, scapegoats were looked for. "Surely," many Germans told themselves, "it could not have been the military that was at fault for the collapse. Even in post-war Germany, the military was the only thing preventing the Bolshevik Revolution from succeeding."

To a large degree, this was true. The military was keeping certain forces at bay and under observation. But it was the military that recommended to the Kaiser that he find a way to end the war. Instead, he abdicated and left his country to fend for itself.

It is really difficult to understand the role the military played in pre-war (and even post-war) Germany. Even in the United States, where veterans hold an increasingly elevated place in society, the armed forces themselves are not held in the same high esteem as they were in Germany. It's almost difficult to overstate its place in society, actually.

Germany, as it was in 1914, was founded around the Kingdom of Prussia, which lay in the northeast of the country. Prussia itself was a rather poor area—its soil was sandy, and its cities were much smaller than most other sizable European kingdoms and principalities.

The first king of an independent Prussia was Frederick I, who realized, despite his love of culture and the arts, that Prussia's position in the center of Europe put it at great risk and began to form what would eventually become the best army on the Continent. His son, Frederick William I, who gained the throne in 1713, disdained the arts but loved the military, and it was he who really formed the military ethos and culture of the Prussian state. Known for his harsh brand of discipline in every area of his life, Frederick William was even known to beat citizens of any rank on the street if he felt they were too slovenly or loud...really, whatever annoying trait struck him at the time. His military became a reflection of his will, and the training of the Prussian Army turned it into one of the toughest, harshest, and most feared in the world. The Prussian Army became one of Europe's first perpetually standing professional armies since the Roman legions. Many of the other nations in Europe had a small core of aristocratic officers or men with some military experience, and when war came, they called for a levy, a draft of untrained soldiers to fill its ranks.

Under Frederick William I and his son, Frederick II, also known as Frederick the Great (who hated his father with an incredible vengeance for the harsh discipline he received at his hands but who kept the discipline in the army), Prussia had a trained and highly efficient army ready to move at a moment's notice.

During his time on the throne, which lasted from 1740 to 1786, Frederick the Great defeated Austria on the battlefield many times. He, in an alliance with England, defeated Russia, Austria, Saxony, and France in the Seven Years' War. In this and all other conflicts, Prussia was greatly outnumbered, but due to their training, discipline, and the ability of commanders to think freely on the battlefield, the Prussian forces achieved one victory after another.

Frederick the Great's adjutant, Georg Heinrich von Berenhorst, summed up the role of the Prussian military quite well, both for his time and for the future: "The Prussian monarchy is not a country which has an army, but an army which has a country."

After Frederick the Great, Prussia, like the rest of Europe, was faced with the once-in-a-lifetime military talent of Napoleon Bonaparte. Like most of Europe, Prussia, too, lost to Napoleon, and it became a satellite state of France.

When Napoleon suffered his defeat in Russia, Prussia and many other nations and kingdoms rose up against him, and after forming an alliance, they forced him to abdicate. When Napoleon returned in the famed Hundred Days' War in 1815, the Prussian forces were instrumental in his defeat at Waterloo. From that point forward, Prussia slowly established itself as the preeminent German-speaking state, though it had rivals in Bavaria and Württemberg.

Beginning in 1862, Prussian affairs were less in the hands of their kings and more in the hands of the famed "Iron Chancellor," Otto von Bismarck, one of the great European politicians of the 19th century. Bismarck's plan, which he began almost as soon as he took office, was to unify the German-speaking states around the Prussian kingdom. By the mid-1800ss, Prussia was becoming an industrial powerhouse, and much of its treasure went to the military.

By 1864, Bismarck and Prussia were ready. In a series of brilliant political moves, Bismarck brought on a war with Denmark, which controlled some northern German states. In doing so, he invited Austria to lay claim to one of these German-speaking areas, as many of the southwestern German states were under Austrian influence or in alliance with it. Bismarck knew that, eventually, he could provoke a war with Austria-Hungary over these states, and what's more, he could make it look like Austria started it. And this is exactly what happened in 1866 when the Prussian Army, which was outnumbered but more disciplined, better led, and well-armed, defeated Austria.

Now, only one nation had some influence over the remaining independent German states, and that was France, which dominated an area along the Rhine River. Once again, Bismarck brilliantly caused another nation to declare war on Prussia. Everyone expected France to win, as they had expected Austria to win. But, as you can guess, they didn't. As was mentioned at the beginning of this book, France was soundly defeated, and Alsace-Lorraine was awarded to Prussia, which was the heart of the newest world power, Germany.

Making all of this possible was the Prussian/German Army. This was a force that was highly disciplined, outfitted with the latest weapons, and flexible enough to allow battlefield leaders to make decisions on the spot.

Looking at all the military had accomplished, it is no wonder the military was held in such high esteem. And it is no wonder that military men, especially officers, particularly Prussian officers, were held in the highest regard. In small towns and villages, military men, even those who were retired, sometimes served as the arbiters of justice and made important decisions on a local level. Men from upper-class and middle-class families wanted their sons to be officers, at least for a time, and many of the young men wanted that as well. Men from lower-class backgrounds had a more difficult time becoming officers; it was rarely done before Hitler's time, but they could at least seek a career as a non-commissioned officer.

As you can now see, not only did the Treaty of Versailles blame Germany for starting the war, making it responsible for paying back the damage caused by the conflict, but it cut into Germany's ability to defend itself and the future of many German men. And perhaps most of all, it impacted the German way of life and its "national honor."

Back to Versailles

Some people on both sides of the Atlantic believed that even with the massive reparations and cessions of land the Germans were forced to make, as well as the reduction of their army, a future war was inevitable. No one (most especially France) believed that the Allies could keep Germany down forever, and many were dubious that Germany would blossom into a modern democracy as many hoped. Hindsight is quite easy, but perhaps the Allies could have implemented a series of conditions for Germany to achieve in order to lessen the burden, or at least gradually increase their military to a reasonable size. But in 1918/19, no one was in the mood to be too lenient with the Germans.

So, by June 1919, the Big Three and their aides developed the final plans for the disarmament of Germany. For a time, some of them wanted a stronger but democratic Germany in the heart of Europe to counter communism, which seemed to be spreading westward in 1919/20. But, with some logic, the French insisted on a weak German military. It was the one thing they essentially would not budge on in all of the negotiations. US President Wilson hoped for an agreement on the disarmament of Europe in his League of Nations, but France threatened to vote against the League of Nations if Germany was not weakened militarily, and the British used the same tactic when it came to naval and some colonial matters that affected them.

So, Germany hadn't even been asked about the terms set within it. The alternative, it was made clear, was the invasion of Germany or at least the industrial heart of it in the west.

Thus, German Foreign Minister Hermann Müller and Colonial Minister Johannes Bell put their names to the Treaty of Versailles in late June 1919.

Under the treaty, the German military was limited to 100,000 men, which was vastly different from its pre-war strength of nearly four million. In the eyes of the Allies, this was enough to control the radical forces in the country but not enough to wage an aggressive war. No tanks were allowed, nor military planes of any kind. No submarines were allowed in the new German Navy, which would only be allowed coastal patrol vessels. The German Navy, as part of the previous armistice agreement, had shipped their fleet to Scapa Flow in the Orkney Islands, which was the home of the British Home Fleet at the end of the war. Hearing that their ships might end up in British hands, the Germans blew them up.

So, France had a weakened Germany that would not threaten an invasion again. They also got Alsace-Lorraine and were going to receive (in theory) millions of dollars in reparations.

But what did Germany get? Or at least what did the Germans feel they got? They got blamed for starting the war, which, technically, they did not. However, a very strong argument can be made that had the "blank check" not been given to Austria-Hungary, World War I would never have happened. Many Germans felt like a child being the only one punished for something their sibling began. They were resentful to the extreme.

When Kaiser Wilhelm II had forced Bismarck out of power in 1909 so he could have the control himself, one of his main goals was ensuring that Germany got its "place in the sun," which has two meanings. For one, Wilhelm wanted to attain colonies in the tropics, like all of the other great powers, and he also wanted to be in a place where the light of glory would shine on a powerful Germany as a strong world power. The Treaty of Versailles, however, stripped Germany of all of its colonies and distributed them to an assortment of the Allied Powers, leading to even more resentment.

Millions of young German men had sought a military career, either for life or for a good number of years. The military provided respect, power, influence, and security. Now, those men were being denied their destiny—their dreams. These dreams coincided with the collective hope of a powerful and respected Germany, in essence, a new country. All of those dreams were wiped out with the Treaty of Versailles. The men who signed the Treaty of Versailles and their political allies became known to many Germans, and not just those on the extreme right, as the November criminals, named for the month of the original armistice.

Money

"Money makes the world go 'round" according to the anonymous emcee in the famous musical *Cabaret*, which takes place in Berlin in the late 1920s and early 1930s. Money indeed makes the world go round, and the lack of it made many people's lives come to a grinding halt.

Though there were many other questions to be addressed in the Treaty of Versailles and its subsidiary agreements, many of which came after the Paris Peace Conference, such as what to do with the boundaries in the Middle East and the creation of the League of Nations, the other main point concerning Germany was how much the Germans had to pay for starting the war.

The reparations question was not settled definitively until some years after the Paris Peace Conference. The Big Three had an amazing number of meetings regarding the issue, many of which were filled with diplomatic and personal threats. Wilson, Clemenceau, and Lloyd George did not get along all that well, and there were literal yelling matches and fake illnesses staged in order to not face another day of seemingly useless talks. To describe the nuances of the negotiations and the beliefs of the Big Three on reparations would be to write a book many times larger than this (please see the sources at the end of this book for an excellent one).

Let's try to sum their feelings up, though. The French wanted to squeeze blood from a stone, and the Americans realized some reparations were necessary but used radically different accounting methods and ideas of "war damage" and "costs" to come up with a much lower figure than the French. The British, meanwhile, were somewhere in between.

All of them knew that demanding too much of the Germans was fraught with peril. They might grind down the German economy and create a breeding ground for communism. They might also force German workers to essentially become "slaves" for decades, as they would, in essence, be paying off their foreign masters, and since their employers would be taxed so heavily, no one would make any money—least of all those on the bottom. There was the possibility that the Germans would simply refuse to pay if the amount was too much, and the Allies would then be faced with the question of whether to occupy the entire country, which would be nearly impossible and cost even more money in the end.

Georges Clemenceau was between a rock and a hard place. Much of his life had been based on his antipathy toward Germany, and his countrymen, who had seen over a million dead and the richest part of their country stripped bare of anything of value, wanted revenge, not only for World War I but also for the Franco-Prussian War. Plainly speaking, the Germans had to pay for what they did to France, and during his time in power, Clemenceau assured his countrymen that they would.

However, as the peace talks ground on, Clemenceau was not so sure that would happen, for a variety of reasons. Firstly, Germany didn't have anything left. Secondly, even if Germany was able to pay something in the near future, it wouldn't be much.

But Germany had to pay something—everyone except the most intransigent and unreasonable of Germans knew this. There were millions of men dead, many of whom were in their prime. And the question the men at the Paris Peace Conference had to face was just how much they were going to charge Germany.

France was determined that they would receive more than the British. They had lost more men, and the war had been mainly fought in their country. Anything the British wanted, the French would want and insist on more.

However, Lloyd George was faced with similar problems. His nation had spent more money than any other country—they had even lent money to France. Of course, that lasted until the British Empire essentially went broke and had to borrow from the United States. The most powerful economy had spent all of its money and burnt through much of its ready credit (although it should be noted that Britain still remained an economic powerhouse—after all, it was a worldwide empire, and its industries were undamaged by the war). The British people, whether they were English, Scottish, Irish, Welsh, or from its Dominions, wanted the Germans to pay, not only because of the costs incurred during the war but the lives lost because of it.

As for the United States, its government loaned both France and Britain incredible amounts of money, and the businesses, banks, and people of that country wanted to be repaid. They had gone to war reluctantly, violating the tenets of George Washington's Farewell Address, and as much as they wanted to see a "new world without war," to paraphrase the sentiments of the time, they also wanted their money back, and many people in the US did not trust the British, French, or Germans.

However, the United States differed from the other two nations in that it had not been devastated as France had been, and they had not lost nearly as many men as either nation. Still, the over 100,000 Americans who died in the nine months of the country's involvement in the war were still worth something, both monetarily and emotionally.

Nevertheless, many Americans followed the lead of President Wilson, who recognized the need of all the Allied nations to receive reparations but wanted to keep them limited. Wilson, like many Americans, also realized that a steep price levied on Germany was likely going to cost more in the end and that it would only cause the cycle of resentment and revenge to continue, which is one of the reasons the Americans were reluctant to enter the war.

When all was said and done, the Big Three could not come to an agreement on the amount. They left that to be dealt with in future agreements hammered out by diplomats, economists, accountants, and political scientists. The Treaty of Versailles itself stated that Germany would be required to pay reparations that would be named at a later date. That later date was two years later in 1921, in the so-called London Schedule of Payments. For the Germans, the pain that began with the armistice continued for three years of uncertainty, and it would only continue.

The initial amount called for in the London agreement was for Germany to pay a series of payments that totaled 33 billion US dollars. That equates to 479 billion US dollars in 2019. This was a staggering amount, yet it was only about a quarter of the initial French calculations (which they knew would never happen). This amount was to be paid off in yearly payments, which would be calculated by a variety of means. One-third of this amount was subject to interest, and the interest began adding up and compounding right away. The other two-thirds would be interest-free and more flexible, as it was based on Germany's ability to pay.

If Germany did not pay on time, sanctions were set to take effect, and the most drastic one occurred in 1923 when the French occupied Germany's industrial heartland, the Ruhr (located in the west, near the French border). In turn, this caused strikes, which were sometimes put down violently by the French, which only further reduced Germany's ability to pay. Additionally, part of the reparations package was not monetary per se. It called for the seizure of all of the coal from Germany's largest coal-producing area, the Saar (also near the French border), for fifteen years. That both took money out of German pockets, which reduced reparations, and it reduced the ability of German industries to get back on their feet since they were powered by coal.

The French occupation of the Ruhr set off a crisis that resulted in further talks on reparations and new agreements. This produced the Dawes Plan of 1924 (named for the American banker and diplomat who chaired the commission that developed the plan, Charles Dawes). The Dawes Plan restructured payments and constructed international loans to help Germany repay on time. In 1928, the Germans asked for even more flexibility, and final reparations payments of 26 billion US dollars (over 394 billion dollars in 2019) were agreed upon. This was to be paid off by 1988. Believe it or not, and even though Hitler stopped all payments, Germany's final reparations payment was made in 2010.

Of course, any economic shock has many effects. The war itself was devastating, taking out many young men from the workforce. But layered on top of that was the reparations payments, the lack of ready cash, the demoralization, and workers being sidelined in the Ruhr by the strike of 1923. This all led to massive inflation. And this inflation was so massive that it has its own name in history: the German hyperinflation of 1923 and 1924.

Reacting to all of the factors listed above and more, the German government unwisely began to print more money in an attempt to "pay" for all of its debts and the salaries of the workers in the Ruhr and its subsidiaries. In November of 1923, one United States dollar was worth over *four trillion marks*. Yes, you read that right. Take a peek at this picture below, which was taken in 1923/24.

Illustration 8: This woman is paying for potatoes with baskets full of cash

Illustration 9: When I was a boy, my father gave me a German hyperinflation bill. I thought he was a millionaire until he explained the truth

Eventually, the German government did take measures to halt the inflation, which was about the same time they were speaking to the Allies about the Dawes Plan. The Allied Powers wanted their money as well (and not the type pictured above), and so, they worked to help Germany get back on its feet. Pressure was put on the French to end their occupation of the Ruhr, which they did—eventually.

The German hyperinflation was more than an economic shock. It was a deeply psychological one too. Germany had developed a social safety net, but it was not enough to cope with the hunger and misery caused by this massive shock. Of course, when times get bad, people want someone to blame. And so, they blamed the November criminals. They blamed the Allies. They blamed the banks and the "international capitalist economic system." Many blamed the Jews, as you can see in this pamphlet cover, which was printed before the rise of the Nazi Party.

This is not the place for a discussion of German/European anti-Semitism. Suffice it to say that, for many reasons, some going back centuries, ignorant people in Europe, as well as North America, have believed that the Jewish people are the central controlling figures of high finance. This prejudice was only made worse when times got bad. Making things even worse was the fact that one of the largest European banking houses, Rothschild's, was run by a Jewish family.

In reading about the rise of Hitler, you will understand that when times got bad, his popularity went up. When they got better or leveled out, his popularity waned. The Nazis and other far-right groups (and those on the far-left as well) enjoyed surges of popularity during the hyperinflation and again in 1929 when the Great Depression began.

Of course, the Great Depression of 1929 had many causes, as well as many other factors that contributed to its duration. Obviously, the flashpoint was the collapse of the stock markets of the world, beginning on Wall Street. Put simply, this was caused by rampant speculation (not only in the US but across Europe) based not on hard facts but on the completely ignorant notion that stocks would keep going up and then borrowing to put money in the market. Companies large and small, as well as investors and banks (which, in addition to loaning people money, also invested in the markets), borrowed to buy stocks. When those portfolios crashed, the debt was still left. And when no one could pay their debts, it set off a chain reaction that affected everyone from the bottom to the top.

So, the Wall Street Crash of 1929 can be considered the tipping point. In the US, bad weather and dropping farm prices, among other factors, contributed to the crash. Other nations had their own unique problems, especially Germany. One problem that contributed to the length and pain of the depression in that country was the reparations required by the Treaty of Versailles.

Making this situation even more bizarre is that by the middle 1920s, many of the hard feelings brought about by the war began to abate, especially in the United States but also in England. The French, located where they were, were a bit more hard-headed, but even some Frenchmen began to at least realize that the reparations were having a deleterious effect not only on Germany but on all of the advanced economies of the world.

When individuals begin to accrue debt and cannot pay it back, they can do two things: declare bankruptcy or get more loans to pay off the original ones. In the case of Germany, the first had essentially been tried during the Ruhr strikes, albeit on a small scale. We saw what happened when that occurred. Bankruptcy would not be accepted as an excuse, and it would only make things worse. So, the Germans were left to borrow more money.

But who could they borrow it from? Britain and France didn't have it. Only one nation did: the United States. So, the Americans and their banks issued new loans to the Germans, who used that money to pay off the British and French, who used that money to pay off the

Americans. And the Americans then used that money to make loans to the Germans. This is a very simple explanation, but the concept does help to illustrate that money was being shifted from account to account and not being invested in anything real, which only helped lead to the worldwide economic crash.

In addition to the economic nightmare were the new boundaries of Germany that were formed in 1919. Aside from the situations of the Ruhr and the Saar, the Rhineland was demilitarized. No German troops were allowed on their own soil, but the worst part of all was the dividing of Prussia, the state that had the foundation stone of Germany itself. Poland, a landlocked nation, was given access to the sea, the Prussian city of Danzig was made a "free city" administered by the League of Nations, and East Prussia was separated from the rest of Germany by a stretch of Poland. Liberal Germans, as well as conservatives and Nazis, seethed at this humiliation.

The Communist Party in Germany (*Kommunistische Partei Deutschlands* or the KPD) and the many extreme-right parties of Germany, including the Nationalist Socialist German Workers' Party (*Nationalsozialistische Deutsche Arbeiterpartei*, also known as the Nazis) benefited greatly from the 1929 crash, as membership went way up in both parties. As such, representation in the state and federal parliaments went up as well. Both the Nazis and the Communists gained popularity by helping feed people on the streets, of which there was more every day. Street urchins were literally eating rats, and crime soared. Things seemed out of control, and when things seem out of control, people turn to someone or something that seems like they know what they're doing.

The Americans were fortunate that person was Franklin Delano Roosevelt for them, but even in the US, extreme parties on both sides gained influence as the Great Depression got worse. For a time in 1931, it seemed like things might slowly level off. But in 1932, the markets crashed again, and not so coincidentally, it was 1932 that marked the high point of Nazi power in free elections. In actuality, in the last election before Hitler was appointed as chancellor by

President Paul von Hindenburg, the popularity of the Nazi Party waned a bit. No matter. Things *seemed* out of control. Hindenburg made the fatal move on January 30th, 1933, when he appointed Adolf Hitler as the chancellor of Germany.

Here is a collection of political cartoons and pictures from a variety of sources in Germany and other countries depicting the results of the Treaty of Versailles and its effects.

Illustration 10: "Germans! Think about this!" A 1924 depiction of the November criminals stabbing the German soldiers in the back. The figures in the background are anti-Semitic stereotypes, but it should be noted that this was not a Nazi cartoon.

Illustration 11: In Austria, which had been reduced in size by the treaty, many on the right wanted a union with Germany; however, this was forbidden by the treaty. In this 1919 Austrian cartoon, a German soldier is being "stabbed in the back" by a Jewish stereotype, years before the rise of the Nazis.

Illustration 12: In an attempt to counter right-wing propaganda, German Jewish organizations, such as the Reich Federation of Jewish Front-Line Soldiers put out cartoons that showed that the Jewish community had fought and died for their country

Illustration 13: Here, Hitler crawls out of the scrolled Treaty of Versailles. By the late 1920s and early 1930s, many people in England and the US began to agree that perhaps the Treaty of Versailles had been too harsh.

Illustration 14: The Big Four leaving Paris. Clemenceau says, "I think I hear a child crying." In the corner is a weeping child, who represents the German draft of 1940. This is an English cartoon printed years before WWII.

Illustration 15: This English cartoon recognizes that Germany under Hitler was rearming. It also lays part of the blame on the Treaty of Versailles and the reparations Germany had to pay. The caption reads, "I never did like that old word."

Chapter 10 – The League of Nations Fiasco

History has not been kind to the Treaty of Versailles and the men who drew it up. Why would it be? It was a key factor in the rise of Hitler and the devastation that followed. But it was not the only reason, and when considering how much of the blame Versailles should be given, it's important to understand a few things.

First, the Allies were working without the benefit of hindsight. Though some did feel as if the terms of the treaty were too harsh on Germany, no one could have foretold the gas chambers of the Holocaust. That was a nightmare centuries in the making, and it was only exacerbated by the Treaty of Versailles and the Nazi propaganda that surrounded it.

Second, given all that you have read in this book so far, what were the Allies to do? They had populations that had been decimated and shocked psychologically, emotionally, and economically (and we all know that economic insecurity causes even more psychic and emotional damage). Had the Allies simply done what was likely the best thing to do and demanded the lowest possible amount from the Germans, perhaps much of the economic turmoil of the next decade and a half would've been eased. The stock market still would have crashed, but perhaps it would not have been so devastating, and surely hyperinflation would not have occurred.

But that simply was not possible at the time. In all likelihood, low payments would have only encouraged Germany to eventually rearm anyway. They were, after all, still the most industrialized and populous nation in Europe. Like a child that gets a smack on the hand for a serious offense, Germany might have figured another try at Alsace-Lorraine was worth it in a decade or two anyway.

Third and finally, the people of France and Great Britain (and to some extent the United States) would not have tolerated it. Politicians who were seen as being "too easy" on Germany would be voted out quickly in upcoming elections.

Wilson Comes Home

Woodrow Wilson arrived in Europe as a messiah. That is only a slight exaggeration. As was mentioned at the very start of this book, crowds of people mobbed him everywhere he went. Pictures of him and his Fourteen Points were everywhere, and plates, buttons, and every kind of collectible you can imagine were made with his image. He and America were the great hope of millions of Europeans. "Self-determination of peoples," which is paraphrased from Wilson's Fourteen Points, was on the lips of practically every European in 1919. If only Wilson had some notion of what that really meant.

It has been said that Wilson lived in an "ivory tower" in his mind, where the dirty business of geopolitical reality couldn't reach. Like many Americans before him, Wilson was an idealist—he believed that the inherent goodness of man could be brought out into the sunlight if it could be led there. Many Americans believed that their nation was fighting not only for the defense of its rights but also for a new future in which democracy and deliberation would be the order of the day.

However, Wilson didn't account for a number of things with this sentiment. First and foremost were the deep historical feelings that ran through the nations of Europe. In just France, for example, there were millions of men and women who could still remember when the elephants of the Paris Zoo had to be butchered for food because of the Prussian siege in 1870/71. Clemenceau was one of them. Forty-three years later, the Germans came back and killed over one million Frenchmen. So, Wilson's plans and pleas for a new world order based on discussion, equal rights, and disarmament fell on many deaf ears. And that was just in France.

Still, there were many in every country that thought the League of Nations might work. World War I had been so awful that almost every alternative had to be considered. So, the League was formed on January 10th, 1920, and had its first meeting six days later in Paris. In November, its headquarters was moved to Geneva, Switzerland, where it met from then on.

When Woodrow Wilson went home, he was a tired man and in poor health. Additionally, he was seen to have given way too much to France and the UK: high reparations, the division of the Middle East, and the German colonies in Africa, to name a few. "What exactly had Wilson gone to Europe for?" is something many Americans (especially Republicans) asked themselves.

In their minds, it was clear the Europeans were up to their same old tricks as before, getting whatever they could. And it was also obvious to them that the average American didn't really profit from the war, although their incomes and the standard of living did rise. Massive wealth was accrued by the big corporations, the ones that made the tanks, supplied the oil, and made the guns and other military supplies. Almost 120,000 Americans died for the Europeans to go back to their old tricks and for (what we might call today) the "one percent," and there was evidence aplenty that these "fat cats," to use the parlance of the time, had overcharged the government and taxpayers to incredible degrees.

When Wilson came home from Europe in June 1919, he went out on a public relations tour to promote the League of Nations and encourage voters to pressure the Senate to ratify the Treaty of Versailles. Already in poor health and tired from his European efforts, Wilson suffered a stroke in October, which virtually sidelined him for the rest of his presidency. Debates have raged since that time over who was truly in charge in the White House, whether it was Wilson himself, his wife Edith, Colonel House (with whom Wilson had a falling out), or a group of people.

By that time, who was in charge really didn't matter in regard to the treaty vote. Henry Cabot Lodge, the Republican leader in the Senate, hated Wilson, and the feeling was mutual. Wilson had made things even worse by not taking any Republicans with him to Paris. After all, the Senate's role in advising and consenting to treaties is spelled out in Article II of the US Constitution, which Wilson ignored completely. Even when Lodge proposed some changes that might get enough Republican votes to pass the treaty, Wilson rejected them outright. Wilson may not have wanted to go back to the British and French with new addendums to be hammered out. He was tired and sick, not to mention that he was an arrogant man who wanted his way.

In March 1920, the United States Senate failed to ratify the Treaty of Versailles and join the League of Nations. Most clear-thinking people in the world knew at that moment that the League of Nations was dead.

In its lifetime, the League had a few accomplishments. Most of them were small economic and political agreements that had only a minor or very localized effect, though, in 1921, it did successfully mediate between hostile Germans and Poles in the division of Upper Silesia, the struggle over which had resulted in savage battles between Polish and German paramilitaries.

Of course, the League is most remembered for its failures, the three largest of which involved the future Axis Powers of World War II. The first serious challenge to the League was Japan's invasion of Manchuria in 1931. These "incidents," as they were called by the Japanese to downplay them, were nothing but naked aggression by ultra-nationalist elements in the Japanese military, and they were completely illegal as far as the League was concerned. But what did the League of Nations do? Nothing. It condemned Japan's actions two years after the fact in February 1933, after which Japan simply and dramatically walked out of the League.

The actions of Japan and the League's lack of consequences were not lost on Hitler, who had come to power in Germany in January 1933. In an overwhelming vote, the German people voted to leave the League in November of that same year. Though it would seem that, considering the nature of the Hitler regime, any vote would be strictly controlled and rigged, this one was not. Most Germans did not want to be in the League from its inception.

In 1935, Italy invaded Ethiopia, then known as Abyssinia, one of only two independent nations in Africa at the time (the other being Liberia). Benito Mussolini, who by this time had been in power for fourteen years, was acting on his nationalist dream of resurrecting a new "Roman Empire" in Africa, as Italy already controlled Libya and Somalia. Ethiopian Emperor Haile Selassie personally went to the League of Nations and made an appeal to the world to aid his country, which was fighting a 20th-century world power with 18th- and 19th-century weapons, all to no avail. Italy, after having its actions condemned by the League, also left it. Mussolini had seen Japan and Germany defy the League of Nations and was sure he could do the same without any real consequences—and he was right.

You might wonder why the League did not interfere in these matters, especially in the cases of Japan and Italy, as clear and unprovoked aggression had taken place. After all, this was the prime mission of the League.

The answer, sadly, is relatively simple. Let's look at one nation and its response. By 1931, the Great Depression was two years old. Great Britain had demilitarized to a great extent after World War I, and even thirteen years after the end of that war, the UK (and most of Europe) was war-weary. The average Briton didn't want to fight in a war that didn't actually threaten them. It had not been all that long since World War I, and so many still vividly remembered how terrible war was. Beside that lies the fact that Britain had significant business interests in the area, especially in Hong Kong, but in other places as well, that would be vulnerable to the Japanese if they decided to interfere. The British also had a worldwide empire to defend, and a sizable portion of that empire was just waiting for the moment the British were overextended to rebel and perhaps gain independence.

Similar questions were asked about Italy's Ethiopian adventure, and in 1936, Italy and Germany were allies and much stronger than they had been in 1919 when the League began. Other nations asked themselves similar questions.

Americans asked themselves the same type of questions: "Why had we even gone to war? Why would we fight thousands of miles away in a place we've never heard of?" By 1931, the year Japan attacked Manchuria, most Americans believed that their entry into World War I had been a mistake, and they were not going to send more young men to fight in a war that didn't really concern them (or so they thought) and likely wouldn't change anything. To them, it appeared that World War I hadn't changed anything.

Also, by the late 1920s and early 1930s, most Americans realized that the Treaty of Versailles had done more harm than good. Some had even begun to believe that Germany had been seriously wronged. Many in the US Navy knew, and had known for some time, that a war with Japan in the Pacific was likely inevitable, but the American people did not—many could not even find Japan and its Pacific island outposts on a map. Even though American sentiment was clearly with China (for many historical reasons too numerous to mention here), virtually no American was going to support a war with Japan, especially with the Great Depression raging at home.

Illustration 16: By 1941, anti-European feelings in the US had developed into the "America First" movement, which Theodor Geisel (later known as Dr. Seuss) was critical of.

Illustration 17: Here, Uncle Sam is concerned that the powers of Europe (France, Britain, Italy, and Yugoslavia/Serbia) are sowing the seeds of future wars

In 1933, one politician summed up the situation caused by the Treaty of Versailles and the reparations that went with it.

> It is not wise to deprive a people of the economic resources necessary for its existence without taking into consideration the fact that the population dependent on them are bound to the soil and will have to be fed. The idea that the economic extermination of a nation of sixty-five millions would be of service to other nations is absurd. Any people inclined to follow such a line of thought would, under the law of cause and effect, soon experience that the doom which they were preparing for another nation would swiftly overtake them. The very idea of reparations and the way in which they were enforced will become a classic example in the history of the nations of how seriously international welfare can be damaged by hasty and unconsidered action.

That politician was Adolf Hitler.

Conclusion

Today, many historians regard World War II not as the "Second World War" but as sort of a "World War I 2.0"—a four-year conflict followed by a 21-year pause in which hatreds continued to simmer and ugly prejudices grew genocidal under economic ruin and perceived international injustice.

Woodrow Wilson died in 1924 and did not live to see the failure of his great dream, the League of Nations. In his defense, it must be said that the United Nations, which came to life at the end of World War II, was built on the foundations of Wilson's idealism as well as its mistakes.

Georges Clemenceau passed in 1929, just after the stock market crash. In the years following the Paris Peace Conference, Clemenceau had come to believe that his successors had blundered in dealing with Germany. They had not coordinated with Great Britain, which, in turn, alienated them. This caused Britain to slowly become more interested in the hostile political environment in France than in enforcing the treaty. Clemenceau also made a highly popular speaking tour in the United States in which he praised the nation but condemned America's decision not to ratify the Treaty of Versailles or join the League of Nations.

David Lloyd George came to believe that the Treaty of Versailles was a mistake. He had argued for milder reparations than the French and had been critical of their move into the Ruhr. He believed that a carefully monitored Germany could be a bulwark against the spread of communism in Europe, but he himself saw the rise of communism in Germany itself in the 1920s. By the early 1930s, Lloyd George was among those in Britain that had come to see Hitler not as an enemy but as a German patriot, who, it seemed at the time, was working miracles in his country.

Throughout the 1920s, elements of the German General Staff, the group at the head of the German Army, had been secretly rearming. This was mainly done by making clandestine agreements with the Soviet Union. When Hitler announced open German rearmament in defiance of the Treaty of Versailles, the wheels had already been in motion for a decade. For a time, Lloyd George and others thought this was only natural; after all, in their minds, the treaty had been too harsh. Lloyd George's close friend, Winston Churchill, differed in opinion. However, by 1937, Lloyd George had come to see that Hitler was increasingly bent on aggression and disagreed with the policy of "appeasement" instituted by Prime Minister Neville Chamberlain. Lloyd George remained in Parliament until his death in late March 1945, but he never held real political power after losing the position of prime minister in 1922 over issues with France.

The Treaty of Versailles, as horrifically consequential as it turned out to be, was a product of its time. The men who worked on it did not blithely put it together. In fact, the leaders and diplomats of the world's greatest powers worked on it virtually non-stop for six months. As the ancient Greeks would've said, "They were between Scylla and Charybdis," or as we say, "Between a rock and a hard place." It's hard to imagine that anyone, given the time and circumstances, could have done much better.

Sources

Blakemore, Erin. "Germany's World War I Debt Was So Crushing It Took 92 Years to Pay Off." HISTORY. Last modified 27, 2019. https://www.history.com/news/germany-world-war-i-debt-treaty-versailles.

Cramer, Kevin. "A World of Enemies: New Perspectives on German Military Culture and the Origins of the First World War." *Central European History* 39, no. 2 (2006): 270-98. Accessed March 8, 2020. www.jstor.org/stable/20457125.

MacMillan, Margaret. PARIS 1919: SIX MONTHS THAT CHANGED THE WORLD. New York: Random House, 2002.

Simms, Brendan. "Against a 'World of Enemies': The Impact of the First World War on the Development of Hitler's Ideology." INTERNATIONAL AFFAIRS 90, no. 2 (March 2014), 317-33

Here's another book by Captivating History that you might be interested in

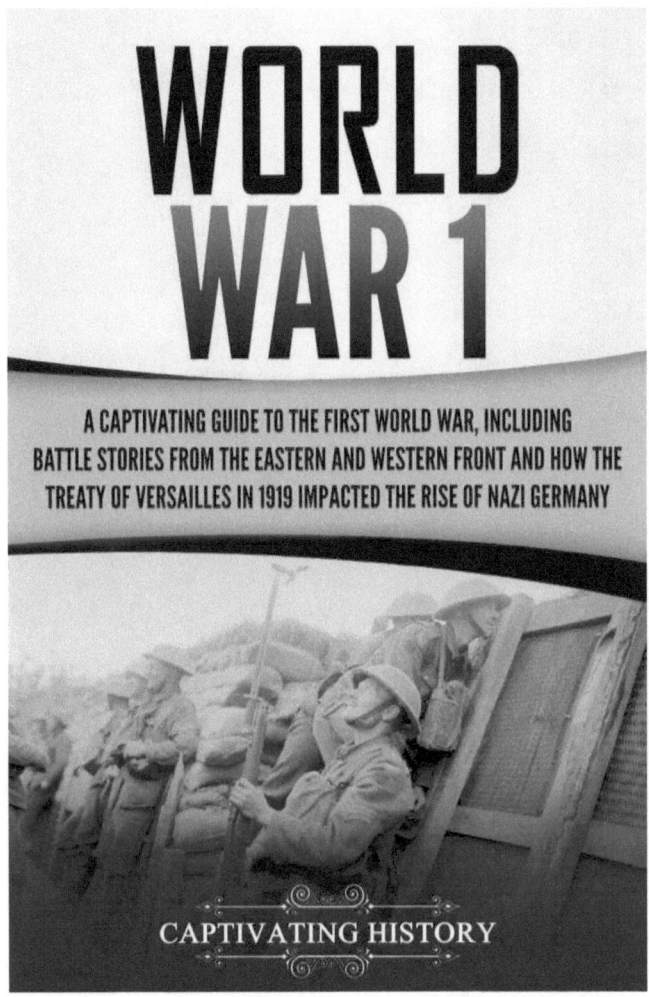

www.ingramcontent.com/pod-product-compliance
Lightning Source LLC
LaVergne TN
LVHW041645060526
838200LV00040B/1723